how to be popular
without losing your mind

Genny in a Bottle

how to be popular without losing your mind

Kristen Kemp

an apple paperback

SCHOLASTIC INC.

New York Toronto London Auckland Sydney
Mexico City New Delhi Hong Kong

To you & me — and
everyone who could
use a genie.

ISBN 0-439-21178-6

12 11 10 9 8 7 6 5 4 3 2 1   0 1 2 3 4 5/0

Printed in the U.S.A.
First Scholastic printing, October 2000

Chapter 1
"Here I Am"
by Genny the Genie

Oh, potato famine! What a curse!

Just when I'm all nice and comfy in my cozy bottle, *it* comes. *It* is the calling — the name I gave to this fantastic feeling I often get. After being in the genie business for a thousand years, I know a calling when I feel one.

Boy, this one was gonna be serious, too. It wasn't a run-of-the-mill, make-me-rich calling, mind you. It was one of those aching kinds. It had to come from someone who *really* needed me. After all, I had gone into genie semiretirement. I was trying not to take the totally tough assignments anymore. I mean, I've been doing this for a whole millennium, so I thought I could take some time off. But that was before this girl, whose name I didn't even know yet, started having this huge personal crisis. I mean, she was in some pretty sad shape! I hadn't felt such intense personal suffering since a little girl

1

named Joan (you know, of Arc) called me, like, almost six hundred years ago. Or was it in the thirteen hundreds? Oh, I don't know — the years become a blur if I think about them too hard.

When the calling comes on, it's so strong that I can never resist it, even if I want to. It's part of a genie's nature, I guess. We genies like to think we can make the world an easier, kinder place for humans. After all, we were once mere mortals, too. So when someone needs me, I go. Pain pulls me forward. Heartbreak is like a magnet.

But that doesn't mean I always want to go — especially on this assignment. I have seen a lot of sorrow in my time, so I needed a break. As much as I love to lend my helping hands, sometimes I need to escape from mental anguish! So I had put down the Rescue Radar Antenna on my bottle (named Throttle) and cut off most of the callings. I spent my days sending e-mails to my genie friends, watching MTV, and reading philosophy to Catfish, my snippy kitty. I could tell that Catfish and Throttle weren't happy with me — they thought I was wasting my time and my talents. But I didn't give a peasant's pea. I mean, I guess I would've been tired of doing practically nothing if I'd been out of it for a few hundred years — but I only got a few short months of relaxation before I got this calling! I could tell this chick *really* needed me. . . .

So back into action I went! Throttle battled the elements — actually, he didn't have to battle much, he just hopped on a bus — and got us to this girl's house. Through his sneaky tricks, which I *still* don't know about because I was stuck in the bottle the whole time, he crawled underneath her pillow.

I heard her sobbing. It was super-duper-mega sad! Immediately, I was back into human-helping mode. I was not only ready for this assignment — I wanted it. I became really antsy to get out and get started — Catfish did, too. It's like dangling our favorite pepperoni pizza in front of us when we're starving, and then not giving us one eensy-weensy bite. We wanted out of Throttle so badly we almost burst.

Come on! Come on! I thought. Just rub your pillow. You have to rub Throttle just once — he's a real stickler about rules. That's what it takes to get me and the cat out of the bag, I mean bottle. And a stroke through the pillowcase would have counted. Ticktock. Ticktock. I was losing all patience — and I don't have a whole lot to begin with.

It seemed like forever, but finally she rubbed her wet face all over her pillow.

Poof! We were released!

Chapter 2
"Why I'm NOT OKAY"
by Nadia

I have never been a freakazoid before.

I don't like it one bit. At my school in Brooklyn, I was just plain old me. I wasn't popular, and I wasn't a dork. Me and my friends made our own crowd. And I think we liked it that way. I mean, we weren't particularly happy or unhappy — we just *were*.

I've been going to this new Midwest school for a month. Here, I'm not even worthy of taking up hallway space. I'm being treated like the biohazard of the seventh grade. People would rather be forced to take pop quizzes than be seen with me, let alone actually be nice to me.

I don't belong here.

My mornings are miserable. My lunches are lonely. And my evenings are unbearable. I am *always* by myself. Even my New York friends' e-mails and phone calls — which come less and

4

less often — don't keep me company. So none of my favorite TV shows are any good anymore, because I don't have anyone to discuss them with. When I just have to get away from the house, there's nowhere to go — except another room. Not having friends is like having a hole the size of a planet in your heart.

I admit it . . . when I first got here, I dreamed of being popular. *Sooo* popular. I thought a girl from New York would be considered funky cool. Instead, I'm a full-on freak — and I don't know why. I mean, these kids call me Knadia from New York because they wondered what I was eating for lunch one day, and I told them it was a knish. They make fun of my music because they've never heard of it before. And for some reason, they just don't seem to like the way I dress. If you ask me, I am fashionable — which, to me at least, means you have to wear lots of black clothes from hip New York stores. But kids at my new school say I look like I want to be a rock star, and that I watch way too many music videos. What the heck is *that* supposed to mean? I'm already worried enough about my looks. If I didn't dress my age, people would mistake me for a nine-year-old. And I'm thirteen! It's hard to be barely five feet tall, and so skinny that kids think I'm a boy. They can rip on my food and my music, but dissing me for how I look is definitely the meanest thing on earth that they could do.

I am smart and into all of the things that were cool at my old school — like writing poetry, listening to rap music, and knowing a lot about movies. Those things just don't fly here, either.

It doesn't help that I've never seen some of the stuff that's popular here, and they've never seen the stuff that's popular where I lived. For example, these girls wear brighter colors than I do. They are also into different kinds of bracelets and necklaces and barrettes than I'm used to. They dance really differently, too. And worst of all, they eat a lot of McDonald's. I'm a vegetarian, and I hate McDonald's.

Then there's the hair! Mine is cropped off really short — my friends used to say it showed off my itty-bitty facial features. We all had pretty short 'dos. Here, though, they all have long hair — really long hair. For some reason, my look is all wrong. My whole life is all wrong right now.

That brings me to my cousin Frieda, who is also in my grade. She keeps telling me that I shouldn't change a thing about myself. But that's because she and her best friend, Matthew, think they're so wacky and different. Sometimes, I think they're just whacked. They are into everything from the eighties, and they like to shop at thrift stores for out-of-style clothes. They love the Cure and all kinds of weird new-wavy music. Were they even born when that stuff was in? Anyway, they don't understand what it's like to be me at all. At least they fit in *somewhere*. They hang out with the Einsteins — they all consider themselves the superior-minded species of the school. Really, though — and I don't mean to be cruel when I say this — they're not even on the map when you're talking about the social stratosphere. Put simply, they're geeks.

And I'm in worse shape than they are.

There's only one other person I have spoken to since I landed on this planet called Indiana. His name is Chris.

Chris.

Heaven is him! Imagine the most adorable and amazing thirteen-year-old boy you've ever laid eyes on. That's Chris. He looks like a movie star — not a plastic, too-beautiful one, but the kind who could be your incredibly cute next-door neighbor. I'm lucky because he *is* my neighbor. So I get to see his freckly, all-American face frequently. I look out my window when he's in his yard and gaze at his sandy-colored soft brown hair. I am mesmerized by his sweet, shy smile — one that he's always flashing. And oh, those kind brown eyes . . .

He has to be a nice boy, too. I just know it. He lives two doors down from my new house, so before my first day of school he came over to say hello to me. We talked for a whole half hour about music and movies. He had heard of some of the bands I like! That was my first visit to heaven. At first, I thought this would be a great new place to live.

But it was torture when he blew me off at school. He would grin and say hello. He'd even make some quiet, Chris-like conversation. But he didn't hang out with me or anything. Maybe that's because he's always with the popular kids on the swimming and tennis teams. (A few of them are the ones who make so much fun of me.) He lunches with the cheerleaders. I've never seen any of them at his house — so I don't know how close they all are. I just know that he doesn't want to be humiliated by Knadia from New York when we're at school.

I can't blame him. What do I have to offer? I'm just a middle-school loser. Meanwhile, he's an amazing person with lots of friends and interesting things to do. I can see why he wouldn't want to hang around with me. *I* don't even like hanging around with me!

So this move is unfair. It's not my thing. It's just turned my life into one big heartbreak after another.

Chapter 3
"I'm So Sad!"
by Genny the Genie

I popped out of Throttle, and she didn't even see me! She was crying so hard and was so immersed in her miserable world that she failed to notice that a genie and a cat were right there in her own room.

Whew. At that moment, I knew for sure that this would be heavy.

I didn't do anything to stop her sadness. I believe that tears help people heal. Sometimes it's better not to interrupt someone when they're in the middle of a cry. Good cries are good for your spirit. If you don't have true sadness, it's nearly impossible to know what it feels like to be happy. At least I've learned those few things in my thousand years on this earth.

After a few minutes, tears stopped coming out of the girl's eyes, but her sobs continued. They were dry and deep, and she sounded like a sad song. I stood there for a while, watching her

9

weep. I've seen so many kids get upset. They are all very different and fascinating. Some kids are loud and angry; some are gentle and soft. Others start to cry even more because they're angry at themselves for crying in the first place.

I watched her even more intently, thinking about the times in my life when I have cried. See, technically, genies can't cry. We feel sadness, but the pain and emotion doesn't feel as deep or as sharp as when you're human. I know. Before I became a genie, I was a thirteen-year-old girl. I've felt that sharpness and cried a million tears to go with it.

If I wasn't a genie, I would have started crying right then and there. I was upset for her, and for all of the kids who I've seen in her very same state. They all have a lot to be upset about. But I have to admit, I was also upset for me. I missed the human life I left behind a whole millennium ago. I longed for my family and friends. I could see my papa's face and feel my mama's hands on my shoulders. I started to shiver. Then I thought about something that brought on a sharp pain that I shouldn't even be able to feel, because I'm not human. That always happens when I think of a boy named Frederick.

Chapter 4
"I'd Like to Introduce You to Matthew and Frieda"
by Nadia

I had to stop sobbing. Frieda and Matthew were coming over, and I didn't want them to see me in such a pathetic state. They were the only visitors I ever got, so the last thing I needed was to scare them off, too. Yes, they were a little strange. But they seemed to like me — and that's more than anybody else did. I looked in the mirror and wiped the tear smears off my face. I jumped because I heard a *thunk* in my closet, but it was probably just Frieda stomping up the stairs.

"What's up, babycakes?" she asked as she breezed into my bedroom. She had recently dyed her hair red with a Kool-Aid packet, and she wore a fluorescent-pink headband that was tied in a bow. I think she liked it when people giggled at her. She was very into doing the unexpected.

"We just thought you might be lonely, since we didn't see you at school today," Frieda said. "It was actually Matthew's idea to pop on over."

"I was in hiding," I replied.

"Oh, why? You're so beautiful," she said as she touched my short hair. All of a sudden, I wished I could belong in Frieda's weird (and sometimes fun) world. She had really made the most of a bad situation — after all, you haven't seen my aunt and uncle. Yes, she was annoying, and she had strange fashion sense. But she was definitely sweet and sincere, too. As for Matthew — God doesn't make guys more kind and thoughtful than he was. He actually had potential to be a total Bradley if he'd just give up the Eastland shoes he wore with those dorky oxford shirts and the vests his mom must have picked out for him.

"You really need to hang out with us more, Nadia," Matthew said.

"Yeah, I know," I lied. I kinda wished I could be closer to them. But truth be told, I was uncomfortable with their constant zaniness. "I'm just trying to adjust to everything."

He kept going: "You really should join in on our new project. We've decided to start an underground secret geek society."

"Yeah!" Frieda chimed in. "We're all gonna meet once a month to discuss issues that are important to the Einsteins. You know, like how to get better at math, how to bargain for better prices at the Goodwill, and how to create a coup to overthrow the popular kids who always get on the student council. That last one is crucial!"

I was speechless. How could I get involved with dissing all things having to do with popularity?

"What do you think?" Matthew asked me, while he adjusted his thick glasses.

"Um, I don't know."

"What do you mean?" Frieda said, wounded. "Wouldn't you like to see geeks finally have some say at school? There are more of us than them, you know. If we band together, we can overcome even the worst middle-school atrocities!"

"Yeah! The next time somebody blows a snot-ball on my liverwurst sandwich, they'll get after-school suspension!" Matthew yelled.

"Matthew, that happened in the third grade," Frieda said.

"Yeah, well, what about when a bunch of snots put that 'Einsteins Eat It' sign on our lockers? That wasn't long ago."

"Okay, whatever. I thought that was kind of funny. Remember? I taped the signs all over our folders."

"Hang on, Frieda, you still wanna have the secret society, right?"

"Sure thing!" she answered. She'd never *not* go along with whatever scheme Matthew had planned. She practically worshiped the ground he walked on.

So they got excited about their society all over again. Quickly, their rantings got out of hand — they were doing high fives, low fives, and making whooping noises. I thought they were going to start rioting right there in my bedroom.

I felt more isolated than ever.

"Stop!" I yelled, despite myself. They both just stared at me. "I'm sorry. I just have a huge headache. Maybe I can come over tomorrow and talk to you two about it." Another blatant lie on my part. "I think I need to take a nap for a little while."

Frieda told me I just *had* to pop by right after school, and Matthew said he'd love to see me. Was that a romance vibe I was getting from him? I could never even consider liking him like that! He's supersweet, just not my type. Besides, I knew that Frieda had a thing for him. She told me about it when I still lived in Brooklyn. She's been obsessing about him for the past three years. What a complicated mess — there was no way I was going over to see them tomorrow. Even though I hated the idea of sitting at home alone.

Finally, after begging me to come with them some more, they left. Of course, I stayed right where I was, knowing that I might start crying again any second. I heard them talking about their plans on their way out — once every outcast at school heard about their secret society, they'd have more members than the honor society! They'd turn the tables on everything — they'd even become more popular than the AYM. That stands for Aspiring Young Models, which is a club at school. Really.

I went back to my room and turned on my stereo. I couldn't have felt more like a misfit. Nothing in my new life was going well — nothing. I blasted my music so no one would hear me crying.

I felt so alone. No one was waiting for a phone call from me. No one wanted to hear about my crushes or crises. No one would even care if I never showed up in that school ever again. All traces of my old life were gone.

I wished I'd never been born.

I began to cry again, this time until my lips turned purple and my eyes were bruised.

Then I heard another *thunk* in the closet.

I looked up.

Chapter 5
"You Can Really Believe Me"
by Genny the Genie

"*Bonjour!*" I said to this pretty and petite sobbing girl. I'd been hiding in the closet the whole time her friends were there. Whew, what a strange pair!

I couldn't help but notice her killer sparkly nail polish. I was eyeing it and about to ask her if I could borrow some. Catfish must've read my mind because he bit me just before I opened my mouth. I flicked his nose with my finger to let him know that *I* was the boss here, not him.

"Girlfriend, you've got a killer room," I said, sort of ignoring her reaction. I mean, her walls were covered with my favorite hip-hop rock stars. I was *sooo* psyched; this chick was cool. "I am really digging this," I couldn't help saying out loud.

Meanwhile, she was breathing hard. You

16

know, doing the whole thing I've seen, like, five thousand times before. She jumped around; she ran her hands through her boy-cropped hair; she said, "Oh, my goodness," about fifty times. All the normal stuff. It usually takes about ten minutes, so I give my clients time. I must admit, I was much more interested in the collage she had made out of artsy magazine pictures to cover her bedroom door.

"Nuh-uh, nuh-uh, nuh-uh," she said over and over. Finally, her hands were placed on her face, and she looked like she was about to scream. That was my cue to step in.

"Don't scream," I whispered. "If you make too much noise, I have to disappear. I'll vanish into thin air, *ma chérie!"*

"Where did you come from? Who are you? *What* are you? Do you know what a nervous breakdown is? Am I having one?"

That's when I told her to sit down, honey. "And please, don't speak. We'll get through this a lot faster if you just let me chat."

"Wait one minute," the girl said. "You came into *my* room, your cat is sitting there on *my* pillow —"

Catfish — with one leg still sticking straight up in the air — shot her a dirty look.

" — so I think I can talk if I want to."

"Score!" I pulled my ponytail higher on top of

my head — a sure sign that I am happy. "You're a spunky one — I like that. This will be so much fun!"

"*What* will be fun? You think *this* is fun? What kind of fairy are you? You think you can just puff into my life and then rule my room?"

"Well, yes. That's what I do best, actually."

"No, what you do best is make unassuming, horribly unhappy teenage girls think they've died and gone straight to some freaky Nick at Nite rerun."

"And you're smart, too. Now you're getting it, *ma belle*. Well, except the Nick at Nite part," I said.

"Getting what? Did I die? Oh, my goodness! Where's my great-grandma? I want to tell her — "

"Whoa! I think you better let me talk."

It took her long enough, but the little cutie-pie finally sat down and shut up. I can't say anything until they've calmed down. After all, they have to let me do some talkin'! I'm a genie — and my clients have to let me do my job, which is to make over their lives. Sheesh.

"Okay, let's just get this over with. I'm a genie," I said, pausing to add an element of drama. "I'm *your* genie. This is my associate here. His name is Catfish, and if he were human his IQ would be one hundred and forty."

"A genie? Come on. Then I'm, like, the Statue of Liberty."

"What? You didn't see the *poof*? Throttle!" I snapped my fingers three times. I like to pull this trick on newbies. With the third snap, I disappeared back into my bottle.

Since she'd already seen me, I was allowed to keep talking, so from inside Throttle, I yelled, "Rub me!" The girl didn't answer, and I was getting impatient. Plus, I'd left Catfish out on her pillow — he wasn't going to be very happy about that. "Rub me, gosh darn it!"

She must've done what I said, because with a quick *poof!* and a bit of smoke, I was back in her bedroom.

"Believe me? I can do it again . . . but I would really prefer not to. It's so bad for my skin to shrink and expand like that."

"I think I'm losing it," the girl said — and I believed her.

"You're not losing it," I said reassuringly. "Let me tell you about myself." This time I didn't let her interrupt. It was time for the genie games to begin.

"My name is Genny, and I'm the Year 1000 Genie. I have been circling this earth for the last thousand years in the hopes of making the lives of thirteen-year-olds — like yourself — a little better. You might notice I'm thirteen years old, too. See, that's how it works. The age at which you become a genie is the age of the people you spend your eternity helping. But I won't go into all of that right now. I'll just tell you this. . . . " I had to take a deep breath; I forget to do that sometimes. "I'm all yours. I'm here to solve your problems. I'll be here for twenty-eight days, so we better get started."

"Why should I believe you? Maybe you're an evil witch who wants to, like, get me into the woods and kill me."

"I am not an evil witch. I'm not a ghost. And I *can't* take you to meet your dead great-grandmother. Maybe I can convince you by telling you my story. I was born in the year 987 in what is now Paris, France. That was the year the great leader Hugh Capet came into power, starting the Capetian rule that would last for four hundred years."

"Huh?"

"They don't teach you that in middle school? Oh, the shame. What do they teach you? Don't get me started. Anyway, my father was a wizard in a time when it just wasn't cool to be one. But my father was stubborn and wouldn't change his wizard ways. That's where I get it from, I'll warn you right now. Papa was teaching me all the things a girl back then wasn't supposed to know — like how to read and do math problems. He was also teaching me Wizardry 101. One day I got caught teaching all the boys how to cast spells so they wouldn't catch a cold or come down with the flu. I was totally showing off by telling them right out in the open and, well, the local bishop caught me. He was steamed. If they had invented the guillotine back then, I think that's where he would've sent me.

"But instead, the bishop decided to make me his maid as punishment for me and my father. But my papa wasn't about to let that happen. He did some dance, and the spirits came to rescue me — I knew they would. I ended up at the Grand Wizard's palace. He told me I had two choices: I could run across the countryside and try to hide, or I could become a witch. I told him neither choice sounded cool to me, so I just hung around his house for a few weeks thinking really hard and trying to make a good decision. Meanwhile, the old Wiz and I got along great! I still miss him. We played and laughed and joked like crazy. Then one day he said to me, 'All right, I've got an idea. . . . I'll make you a genie. You're smart, sincere, and sweet. But this is a very big position — there's only one genie appointed every hundred years. And this year is an extraordinary year. The Year 1000 Genie has to be special. I've given it a lot of thought — I think you'd be perfect.' So *boom*! I became a genie. I got A-pluses in all of my genie classes. The rest is history. Literally. So what do you say?"

"You could be making all of that up! Speak French!"

"Oui. Le Big Mac. Le Big Mac. Need more?"

"Yes."

"Well, you know Abe Lincoln? When he was your age, he almost quit studying to become a chicken farmer. Guess who got him back on track?"

"No way . . . "

"Yes! I swear! And you know Florence Nightingale? She wanted to be a vet before she met me!"

"Oh, my goodness. What about your cat?"

I gasped. "That's, like, the hugest secret. I can never tell you that!"

"Oh, *well, then.* Just keep him away from me — I hate cats," the girl said. She took a few minutes to think. "I am so shocked. I am so shocked."

"Do you believe me, then?"

"I don't know." She paused. "I think so."

"Then tell me your name, please."

"It's Nadia."

"Well, I'm glad we've got that settled," I said. I got down on my knees in front of her and bowed my head in the polite old-world genie style. I reached out to put my hands on her knees.

"I am Genny. And for the next twenty-eight days, I'm your genie."

Chapter 6
"What Nadia Wants"
by Genny the Genie

What happened next wore me out. Nadia started going a mile a minute.

"So I get three wishes? I don't know what to wish for! Should I be noble and wish for world peace, or should I just go for it all and ask to be a VJ on MTV? Or maybe I should demand five thousand dollars! Genny, what do you think?"

"I think you better slow down, showgirl. It doesn't work like that."

Nadia wasn't listening to me. She was still all happy trying to figure out what to wish for. She seemed to think I could just snap my fingers and make things magically appear. She was wrong — there are so many misconceptions about genies. It takes all of my time and energy to straighten them out.

"Hey there! Yoo-hoo! Your genie wants to speak. . . ."

"Yeah."

"It just doesn't work like that," I explained again. "I hate those terrible movies like *Aladdin*. They really give the world a completely wrong idea about genies. I can promise you, you don't get three wishes. I am not a magician. I can't make things appear that aren't there."

"Then what *do* you do?"

I could tell she was disappointed, so I snapped my fingers twice. "The manual," I told Throttle. He spit out a thin yellow book, and I handed it to Nadia. "Read it — out loud."

She dusted it off with her fingers, studying it for a second. " *'Your Guide to Genny the Genie.'* " Nadia turned the page. " 'Congratulations, you've just found your first genie. Enjoy! You are a rare and special person who just might need some help. If you use this manual right, you are bound to get it. There are some rules, though. Genies have strict regulations they are required to follow. Some of the more established ones are even allowed to have a few quirks. Good luck! Happy genie-ing!' " Nadia glanced up at me with a weird look.

"Keep going," I said.

" 'Number one: Your genie must obey you at all times, but your requests have to be within reason. Number two: As a general rule, genies cannot do mean things. They can be mischievous, but not mean. Number three: In some

25

cases, your genie has the right to disobey your commands. Number four: You must always remain fully dressed around your genie.' Do I have to keep reading this?"

"Uh, yeah! Do you want me to be your genie?"

" 'Number five: Genies do not do homework or make beds or clean bathrooms. Number six: You cannot tell more than two people about your genie. If you spill to more than that, she will automatically disappear. Your genie will be invisible to everyone besides you and these two people. Don't worry, your parents cannot see or hear her unless you want them to. Number seven: You have twenty-eight days to spend with your genie. After the allotted time, she will disappear. Number eight: Your genie cannot do much magic — but she can work with you and make magical things happen. Number nine: You must provide rubber bands and/or Q-Tips upon request. Number ten: Your genie does not eat health food — please provide pepperoni pizza at least once a week.' That's the end."

"Do you have any questions?" I asked her.

"Yeah, why the Q-Tips?"

"I can't tell you that. Next question . . ."

"Well, I have a problem with the pepperoni. I'm a vegetarian."

That really ticked me off, so I grabbed Catfish

and made like I was getting back into Throttle. "I'm outta here, then."

"No, wait! I guess we can work something out."

"You swear you won't slip me any of that veggeroni junk?"

"Okay, I swear."

"Good. Then we're all set. Now, you have to tell me your problem." I hoped it would be about friends and romance and relationship stuff. Those are my favorite subjects to tackle. And since I've been at this genie gig for such a long time, I usually get sent the projects I'll like. I *sooo* hate making people millionaires. And I'm getting too old for the heavy, save-the-world kinda stuff.

Anyway, Nadia went on to tell me all about her miserable life.

And it *was* pretty miserable. She went from being this happy, well-liked person in Brooklyn, New York, to being an outcast in the Midwest. I agreed with her. This was a major bummer. But even worse, she was all smashy-hearted over a guy who was sweet when they were one-on-one but turned totally snotty when they were at school. The only friends she had were sweet but not her type. (I had seen them — I wasn't sure they were anyone's type but each other's!) They drove her crazy and, even worse,

27

cramped her style. She was sad and lonely. Nadia needed friends.

"Well, your first dream has come true," I told her. "You have a friend. A very loyal, devoted, and *très* cool one, I might add. Consider me your alter ego. . . . your constant companion . . . your best friend on the face of this earth!"

"Really?"

"Yes. What else do you need? I hear you telling me that you're ultra-unhappy. But what about what you want? That's why I'm here. I'm going to help you make your dreams come true — or at least I'll chip my fingernails trying. Just so you know — I have a more than stellar track record. Most kids are very satisfied with my work. I'd be glad to give you references."

"Don't be silly," Nadia said. "I totally trust you — I think. And I don't have to think about what I want. That's easy — I want to be popular. I want to have three thousand friends and be worshiped in the middle-school hallways. I want to be the center of the seventh-grade universe. And there's another thing I want more than everything else put together."

"And what is that?" I asked, but I already knew the answer. She wanted a boy. Hey, I'm a pro.

"I want this guy named Chris to fall madly,

hopelessly in love with me!" She smiled that dreamy I'm-in-love smile at me. "Or at least be my good friend."

"Oh l'amour, oh l'amour, c'est très simple, chou chou."

"English, please. Hey, I command you to speak English from now on."

I gave her a dirty look. She *was* a sharp cookie — I had to give her that. "I said something to the effect of: 'Oh, love, love. That will be a snap!' And don't worry, I can handle popularity, too. That will just take a little bit more work."

"Oh, really?" She was jumping up and down again.

I took a moment to admire her short hair. (Mine is megalong and thick. It's dirty blond and slightly wavy in warm weather — I've never had the nerve to cut it.) I wasn't digging Nadia's makeup, though. She was wearing way too many dark colors. It didn't do a thing for her — she was hiding her pretty blue eyes and rosy cheeks. I better get on that. I'm not very into makeup — except for shiny pink lip gloss. I like to look *au naturelle*; it suits my on-the-poof lifestyle. Besides, I'm French — we take pride in what nature gave us. I think Nadia should, too. As for me, I was given peach-colored creamy skin with freckles and sparkly brownish-green eyes. I'm not a beauty queen genie with lots o' curves, but I'm cool with what I've got.

I *was* dying to raid Nadia's closet, since she and I were almost the same size. But I didn't know if that would be a good idea. She was very urban, and I wear lots of modern wispy girlie clothes, mostly stuff I've collected from my favorite stylish clients over the past hundreds of years. I'd wear my more ancient stuff, but it has turned to rags. Still, I go for a vintage look most of the time. After all, I have a genie image to live up to!

"I am so amazed! I want to get started right away," Nadia said. "What do I do first?"

That was my cue to get to work. "Let me take a look in your closet!" I started to think that this job would be a snap. . . .

Ha!

Chapter 7
"My First (Horrible) Day as a Genie Owner"
by Nadia

We didn't get very far last night. My new genie was just too exhausted. In a frantic whirlwind, she chatted her ponytail loose while she raided my closet. I was so happy — we had everything in common. It wasn't like talking with Frieda and Matthew. I didn't have to try to make the conversation flow. It was more like magic. We totally bounced off of each other — discussing the latest videos, books, and even poetry. She likes Judy Blume as much as I do. She even told me that she had met my favorite poet, Christina Rosetti! She is like my idol. Genny had so many amazing stories, I could have talked to her for weeks without stopping. I'm in awe of Genny — I'm addicted to my genie!

She *is* a little strange. While we were talking, she spastically hurled clothes from their hangers to the floor. Then all of a sudden, she was silent. I looked at the huge pile of shirts, skirts, and jeans and was shocked to see a conked-out, snoring genie on top of them. I watched her in amazement. Every breath she took was fascinating to me. I mean, I felt luckier than a lottery winner.

Though I have to admit that I cringed when her scary brown-striped cat crawled into the pile and purred like crazy. It sounded like he was spitting up all over my stuff. But I guess I shouldn't complain.

I decided last night: Happiness is a warm genie. I couldn't believe it — I went to sleep feeling cheerful, even though the day had started out badly. For the first time in months, I was actually looking forward to going to school.

But when I got up, she wasn't there. I heard her laughing from inside her bottle. I picked it up to rub it, and she yelled, "Don't you dare touch Throttle! I'm watching a killer episode of *The Simpsons*."

I rubbed it anyway; she was so peeved.

"You are evil! *Evil!* I come here to save your sorry life, and you can't even let me watch *The Simpsons*? The nerve of you Americans!"

I walked over to the television in my room and turned it on. Her show was still on —

which I knew because I watched the reruns every morning, too. She looked at me with a goofy whoops-I'm-sorry smile. I said, "I just thought you'd be more comfortable on my bed than in that bottle."

"Oooh, um . . . *merci*," she said. During the next commercial she spoke again. "Thank you again. I wanted to tell you I had a great time getting to know you yesterday. We're going to have a good time together."

"I hope so, I could use one."

"Um, Nadia, do you think you could round up some pizza?"

"Right now?"

"Um, yeah."

"It's seven in the morning!"

"Oh, but I'm dying."

"I promise I'll bring you a fresh pie after school. Restaurants around here don't open until later. I will even get extra pepperoni for you and that thing with fur."

"Hey, watch what you say about the flea-bag," she said. Catfish lifted his nose in the air and walked away while we laughed. He scratched his nails on everything — obviously creating a lot of drama just to get under my skin. I guess he didn't think our comments were funny. Genny seemed to like teasing him.

The Simpsons went off, and we giggled the

whole time I put on my dark eyeliner and black clothes. I was dying to talk to Genny more, but I heard the blare of really bad country music in the driveway. My aunt Pat — Frieda's mom — was outside, with Frieda in the station wagon. She took us to school every morning with bright pink rollers in her hair — thankfully, I got to ride the bus back home. I hated driving to school with Frieda and Aunt Pat every day. They talked about making casseroles, eating them, and then freezing the leftovers. It was the same conversation every morning. "Frieda, would you like eggplant or egg casserole tonight? I think I'll stick with eggplant, if you don't mind, honey. I've had terrible gas and heartburn this week."

I was feeling so good that morning that I didn't get bogged down by the curlers or the conversation. I was in my own wonderful world. I was going to be popular. Chris was going to ask me out. All of my dreams were going to come true.

I didn't just walk to my locker that day — I strutted. I didn't bother to stress about being seen with Frieda, either. I could almost ignore the fact that she was walking beside me wearing a pink oxford shirt with the collar turned up. Her stretch pants were lime green, by the way. Regardless, I still felt almost cool. I had a genie — no one else at school could possibly be so blessed.

I opened my locker to put in my backpack and get out my *Get Healthy and Have a Happy Life* book for homeroom. I heard a group of guys whispering behind me. I thought, *Yes! It's working already. They're here to flirt with me. They're here to fall madly in love.*

Then I heard a snide giggle, a snicker, and a "Look — it's Brooklyn."

"What's going on?" I turned around to say. They stood there silently, not looking at me. Next they walked off, confusing me and making me lose all of my newfound self-confidence. As I walked down the hall, kids kept going, "Chirp, chirp." They weren't really looking at me, but they were giggling those sneaky, mean giggles that tell you something not nice is going on. It was definitely killing my new I've-got-a-genie-and-you-don't attitude. I started feeling like a freak again.

This went on for four periods, until lunchtime. That's when Matthew came up to me, touching my back. I shivered because of the whole romance-vibe thing, then he spoke.

"What? Is this a new fashion statement? Did you know you have a whole bunch of feathers taped to your back?"

I ran to the bathroom and ripped them all off.

Now I'm just plain old "Brooklyn," the new kid who looks like a bird?! I didn't know whether to cry or find the boys who were at my locker that morning and peck their eyes out. I knew I was short and birdlike, with my skinny legs and pointy nose. But make fun of me? How cruel. I was raging — I banged on the bathroom doors and began to cry despite myself. Life was still the same: Unbelievably Unfair.

After school, I burst into my room, ready to turn on the stereo, collapse on my bed, and cry again. Oh, but believe me, I was giving my genie a piece of my mind first. How dare she tell me she's going to save my life when all she really planned to do was wreck it.

I burst into my bedroom — and was stunned speechless. Genny was dressed just like me — in a tight black T-shirt with black pleather pants. She had her hair all pinned up so it looked really short. My makeup was everywhere — on the dresser, the bed, and even the floor. She had obviously tried it all on. Even her cat was playing with my stuff. He had my favorite black scarf tied around his belly — it looked like Genny had put mascara on him. To make things worse, my CDs were all lying on the bed in piles. They were all out of their cases — and some of them were sticking out from underneath the bed. I had no idea what to say except "This day could not possibly get worse."

"Oh, *ma belle*! Whoopsy doopsy! We didn't expect you home from school for a few more hours. And, well, we haven't been out of the bottle for a while . . . so we're having a bit of fun with our research."

"This is a mess! My life is a mess! You're ruining it!"

"I'll clean it up, I promise. I'll have it done in half an hour."

"You can't clean it up! You can't clean up my life! It's worse than ever. I thought you were here to help me out. You're just making things worse!"

"Listen, honey, it's no big deal. I can clean up this mess. But can I keep this necklace? Pretty please?"

"Nothing is serious to you," I said sternly — it was hard to keep quiet because I was steamin', but I didn't want anyone to hear me. I was really in a tizzy. "You show up and tell me how everything is going to change. You make it sound like all of my dreams are on their way to coming true. Well, you know what happened today? Do you know? I got feathers taped to my back! I got chirped at all day! You wanna know why? Because I'm still the biggest loser in school! I'm still a freak to these kids, for no reason — just because I'm new here and I'm different. And the whole time I'm being tortured at school, you're playing dress-up in my room. You're acting like you came here for you! You told me you came here for *me*!" I started crying while I threw the clothes back into my closet.

"I guess this is a bad time to ask you if you brought us some pizza. . . . " Genny had some nerve.

"UGGGHHH! I DIDN'T BRING YOU PIZZA! I HAD A FEW OTHER THINGS TO THINK ABOUT TODAY!" I was losing it. And she wanted pizza.

Genny rattled a mile a minute in French. I just got more and more annoyed.

"Will you speak English?!" I yelled despite myself.

"I'm so sorry, please forgive me. I don't mean to be all about me; I just get carried away. I am so happy to be out of this bottle — and I really like you. I was getting so excited and having so much fun. I was going through your stuff so I could be your own personal fashion consultant."

"Now something's wrong with my looks, too! You are so mean."

"I am not mean. Genies aren't mean! Especially me! I have never been called mean before!"

"You're not, huh? But I made my wish! You were too busy sleeping on my stuff last night to make my wishes come true! You didn't even take the time to wiggle your nose or snap your fingers or rotate your hips or something!"

"Hmph! That's enough! I do not make changes overnight. I am not capable of much magic — I told you that! You people are so instant," she huffed. "Just like Barbra Streisand a hundred years ago . . . Oh, wait, it wasn't that long ago. Anyway, she wished to be a huge star and to have a voice like an angel. She had the biggest hissy fit when she didn't start singing the very next day. Actually, she had a lot of hissy fits. But anyway, getting her voice in tune took a huge amount of work! We went through twenty-eight days of incredibly intensive training. And, well, it worked."

"What's this got to do with anything? I hate Barbra Streisand."

"This has nothing to do with *her*. I'm just saying that I can't make you popular overnight. I can't make a guy love you overnight, either. We have to do some slaving. But stick with me, I swear we'll start making popularity progress in just a couple of days! Be patient — you didn't discover the genie express. You did discover an expert, though."

I didn't know what to say. I just wanted to cry. But I decided not to, because I was a little tired of crying.

"Did that boy talk to you today?"

"Are you kidding?" I asked, swallowing the lump in my throat. She wasn't making me feel any better just yet. "I had feathers all over my back. Would *you* talk to me?"

"Well, I would . . . I have to, you're my master."

"So tell me what to do. Please, Genny!"

"I will, I promise," she said. "But can you get me a pizza before we get started?"

Chapter 8
"You Won't Believe What I Can Do"
by Genny the Genie

Nadia thought my ideas were crazy. I wanted her to wear different shoes, take off her makeup, and watch *The Simpsons* with me. Okay, so I didn't know how those things would work, either — I was just trying to buy some time while I did some brainstorming. I guess she didn't quite fall for it.

I asked her to trust me — you know, to just go with the flow. She looked at me with uncertainty. Then I made the mistake of saying, "You can bet your social status on it, I promise."

She said, "But my social status isn't worth anything."

Oops, I wish I would remember to think before I speak. I changed the subject. I needed pizza. Thankfully, no one was home yet, so we went into the kitchen and found a frozen one. It

41

wasn't pepperoni — neither Catfish nor I were one bit happy. But all things considered, we decided to hush up and take what she had to offer. The whole time she fixed it, she complained that much to her vegetarian dismay her family had a thing for sausage — and bacon and bologna. I told her that I would definitely be in carnivore heaven. Then I ate the pizza like it was the best thing I'd ever tasted in my whole life. I tossed a few pieces to my cat, who sat on the table right next to me. Nadia was clearly not pleased about that. I couldn't help it, I started to squeak while I ate. I do that when I'm in heaven — I don't know why, it just comes naturally to me.

"Don't you eat very often?" she asked, leaning on the gaudy Formica table that had chrome around the edges.

"Oh, no, genies aren't human. The only time we get hungry is when we're out of our bottles. When you shrink as much as we do to fit into a bottle, you don't have much of a stomach, let alone an appetite. We really don't get the munchies."

"Don't you get lonely?" she asked.

"I try not to think about that. A genie's life is to make other people happy, that's all. I just try to amuse myself — Catfish helps me when he's not driving me crazy. I try to make it impossible to have time to think about how lonely I am." I was nervously twisting my thick hair into knots with one hand while I stuffed my face with the other.

She changed the subject. "Do you get bored?"

"Well, sometimes. But time is a human thing. I mean, a thousand years have gone by faster than a horse and buggy."

"Wait a minute. Did I miss something? Horsebuggies aren't fast."

"Your perspective is so twenty-first century. Modern movement for the masses is a relatively new phenomenon. Oh, never mind. When I'm in my bottle, a year feels like a second and a century feels like three days. When I'm out of the bottle, though, I feel the days just like you do. That's when I'm aware of time." I stopped to enjoy the sausage, closing my eyes and licking my lips. "And that's when I get famished! It's just that I miss eating so much. I don't suppose you know how to make swine 'n' carrot stew, do you?"

"Uh, no . . . sorry."

"Fresh goat cheese?"

"Nope! But we have the kind from the store."

"Oh, no, that won't do." I wiped my mouth with the back of my hand, and Catfish licked his paws.

"Would you like a napkin?" Nadia asked.

"Oh, sure. I do forget my manners. I just can't get used to napkins. It took me hundreds of years to figure out utensils!" That was *so* the truth. My manners embarrass me sometimes.

We walked back up to Nadia's room. I was so excited about everything. And I continued to pretend I knew exactly what I was doing. Nadia didn't seem convinced.

"Okay, what do we do now?" she asked me.

I didn't speak — I just got out all of her teen magazines, ripping out the pictures I liked. I told her to wait a few seconds, then rub my bottle. I snapped my fingers three times, and into Throttle I went. I buzzed around inside while Catfish meowed his annoying head off.

"Rub me! Rub me!" I yelled.

Nadia picked up the bottle and held it to her ear. I was quiet, so she went ahead and rubbed it. I emerged with a huge stack of the coolest clothes ever, if I do say so myself. I used colors other than black, which I knew Nadia wouldn't be so sure about. But they were very much like what kids wore on the hippest television shows. I gave her striped tank tops and miniskirts, funky pants, and strappy sandals. Nadia just stared in amazement — for her, I'm sure this felt like her own personal shopping spree.

"Where did you get those?" she asked.

"Didn't you just see me? They came out of Throttle."

"I thought you said you couldn't do magic."

"Oh, I can't. I made them. That's why I was looking at your magazines and your closet. I've had a lot of spare time, so I've practically become a fashion designer."

"You made all of those in two minutes?"

"Well, I told you, when I'm in the bottle, human time doesn't count. I really have no idea how long it took — but it was lots of fun. Exhausting, but fun. I did a fab job, if I do say so myself."

"No way. *You* made those? I am so impressed!"

"Well, try 'em on, girl-*amie*. I think you look way too citified for these smaller-town folks. I picked out some more universal, drool-worthy outfits. And I made sure they'd be your perfect size."

"But they're so colorful!"

"Color can work wonders. Have you ever seen a rainbow? Besides, you have to wear 'em if you want to be cool here. Come on, give 'em a chance. I know you'll look supercute."

I was right, she did. She was wearing little flowered dresses that were a tad tight. I put her in tank tops and skirts. If you ask me, she was one pretty darlin'! She didn't even look too upset about the pinks and reds and purples.

"Now for your hair!"

"My hair? It's short, what can you do?"

I did a lot. I styled it all cutesy and put some sparkly insect barrettes in it.

"Where on earth did you get those?" she asked.

"England, seventeenth century. They were Queen Elizabeth's. And you can only wear them if you promise to pretend that you're a queen, *ma chérie*. Because that's what you are. I just need those back before I leave."

"Oh, my goodness," she said while she touched them. Her eyes looked up at the ceiling and I thought her imagination must be running wild. I knew what she was thinking. I mean, I've seen movies about the queen. Elizabeth had a cute boyfriend and every man in the world wanted to marry her. I wonder if Nadia wanted to be popular like her.

"She was *the* most amazing monarch the British ever had, you know. Something about her was wise beyond her years. Those barrettes were Elizabeth's mother's. Anne Boleyn wore them before she got her head chopped off. You can imagine why Lizzy had a few issues when she was thirteen."

I couldn't help it, I went on to give her a history lesson. I expected her to say, "Come on! Get on with it. Make me popular!" But she didn't. She looked astonished at my stories, and she clung to my every word. I could get used to Nadia's genie worship.

"Now, there are a few rules to popularity, Nadia," I finally said. Then I told her she had to hold her head high — if she thought she was cool, other people would think so, too. She said that sounded too easy. I insisted that it would work.

"What else do I have to do?" she asked.

"Tell me why you want to be popular so badly."

"Because popular girls get all of the privileges. They get the guys they want — guys like Chris. They also get special treatment from teachers. They are the pets. They have fun, too, because they have the best parties. And what is it about popular girls that makes them so pretty? And the ones I want to be friends with, they're always smiling and laughing and holding one another's hands. They never ever seem lonely. Like this one girl, Gretchen, she's the prettiest, sweetist, and smartest one. I want to be best friends with her."

"If you think she's really that sweet, she's worth being friends with," I said. "Do you think you'd want to be friends with her even if she wasn't popular?"

"Definitely."

"Okay, good. One other thing: Don't you know you're pretty? And really sweet, too?"

"No, I'm not. I'm a freak."

"That's your first problem. You have to be self-confident. I am telling you, *you're* pretty and sweet, and I'm never wrong about these things. *Ever.*"

"Yeah, right. I bet you said that to Barbra Streisand, too."

"No, I don't lie. I told her the truth — that she was incredibly talented. And I'm telling you that you're incredibly nice. And you're lucky that you have good looks, too. Now believe it."

"Why?"

"Because I only come to visit special people who have a purpose in this world. I don't know what yours is, but I know you have an important contribution to make. Within five minutes, I knew it was because of your kindheartedness."

"Do you mean I'll be famous one day?"

"Quite possibly — for something or other."

"Can you tell me now? What will I be famous for?"

"I don't know. I'll find out when you do. But you shall be someone special . . . mark my words — I haven't been wrong in one thousand years. If you can't take confidence from that fact, then I can't help you."

"Me? Famous? No way," she said. "I guess I'll try, then."

I was having success, so I went on with the instructions. I wanted her to walk up to Gretchen and say hello. I even told her what to talk about. It sounded like they both enjoyed writing, so I told Nadia to start with that subject. She should ask Gretchen all about the school newspaper, since Gretchen was the editor. I told her to offer to work with them after school so she could learn the ropes. That sounded scary to Nadia, but she said it was doable. She had always wanted to start a school literary magazine anyway, so maybe Gretchen could help her out with that.

Second, Nadia needed to make friends with Gretchen's friends. That would be harder. I suggested she start by going, "Oh, hi!" every time she passed them in class. Then she should walk away as if she were better than them. I assured her it would intrigue them if she held her head high and acted like Queen Elizabeth. After a few days of that, it would be easier for Nadia to initiate some real conversations — without feeling intimidated by them.

Two other things I told Nadia to do may have seemed strange to her. I instructed her to keep a fresh red rose in her locker at all times. I also wanted her to stop eating microwaved food.

When she asked me why, I said, "Just do it!"

"What about Chris?" she asked.

"Be a master at the game of popularity first. Then Chris will be begging you to go out with him! I promise. Patience is a virtue, girl-*amie*."

"This all sounds good," she said. "But will any of it work?"

"I hope so," I said. "I'll give you a boost. Why don't you get me some cereal — with sugar, please — while I — " All of a sudden, my cat screamed and ran. "Get over here, Catfish!" He hid in the closet, but I fished him out.

"What is going on?"

"I need a few whiskers from him — and he isn't too thrilled to see that I'm about to yank them out. I also need a tea bag and some boiling water. Could you get me those things?"

She boiled the water, found the cereal and some tea bags, and brought them back to the room. I had some whiskers in my hands. Catfish was whipping his tail furiously, eyeing me like I was doing something wrong.

"Shhh!" I said to Nadia. Then I strategically started speaking some really weird French. "I need you to turn around — if you watch, it won't work."

The lights flickered. Nadia freaked out — but she kept quiet because she thought I knew what I was doing.

And I did.

I hummed and did weird stuff for a little bit longer.

"Cupcake, I'm all done! And I'm exhausted," I said.

"What did you do? Voodoo?"

"Oh, my wizard's wonder, I can't believe you'd call that voodoo. Hmph!" I replied. "I just did something my daddy taught me. Hey, don't knock it — those ancient spells really work."

With that, I opened the closet door and fell over into Nadia's pile of old clothes. I started snoring within five seconds, hoping she'd think I was fast asleep. Really, I was quite proud of my confidence-boosting scam. It's always the same — humans never fail to fall for, and believe in, a fake spell or two.

Chapter 9
"Meet Ms. Me"
by Nadia

I am telling you right now, everyone should get a genie.

I walked into the junior high looking fly. The barrettes in my hair were the most killer part of my clothing ensemble. Who wouldn't feel at least five feet seven with Queen Elizabeth's jewelry tangled in her tresses? I know I did. And tailor-made designer clothes? I bet no one outside of Soho was sporting those. Except *moi*, that is. How could I not look great when I had my own personal genie stylist?

If I had many more days of this, I'd need my own star on Hollywood Boulevard. And believe me, after my bummer month, I had earned such an honor.

During the entire ride to school, Frieda kept saying, "The look is so you! You are so beautiful!"

They really don't make chicks any sweeter

than Frieda. Even if she hated my outfit — and I'm sure she did — she didn't show it at all. She just beamed at me, making me feel really cute and special. It was nice to feel that way — like someone cared about me. I'm sure she knew it meant a lot to me, since I couldn't stop smiling and saying, "Thanks!" and "Oh, thank you!"

Of course, I told her she looked good, too. I wanted to give her a boost even though the poor girl had dyed her hair with grape Kool-Aid, making it a sick purpley-red brownish color. I'm not against wacky hair colors — but a professional dye job might have been a better idea.

In the car, she also mentioned the secret geek society again while my aunt went, "Yeah! Yeah!" Oh, excuse me, it's now *Secret Geek Society* — with capital letters — because they have formally banded together and applied for official school recognition.

Frieda begged me, "C'mon, Nadia. Please join. We need you."

Oh, my goodness. I wasn't quite sure how to get out of it. But then I honestly freaked and accidentally-on-purpose changed the subject.

"Frieda! Oh, no!"

"What? What?!" she said sensitively.

"I forgot something I need today." We were already walking inside the school at this point, so I couldn't exactly ask Aunt Pat to stop by the gas station or anything.

"Your homework? Act sick right away! That way you can turn it in tomorrow without losing any points. You don't want to ruin your grades."

"No, no. It's nothing like that," I said. Frieda really knows how to overreact sometimes. "I just need a red rose."

"Why? Is there something going on that I don't know about?"

How was Genny's magic supposed to work if I didn't even follow her instructions? I was sweating and pacing, all worried that I would ruin her spell or something.

"Are you okay? Can I do something for you?"

"No, I just need a rose really bad."

"Well, where would you get one?"

"I've seen them at the gas station across the street. Do you think I can make it over there?"

"Why do you need it?"

I panicked, looking her dead in the eye. What was I going to say? "I, um — "

"Wait, don't tell me. I can tell that whatever it is, it's a secret you need to keep. I respect that. I will run and get it for you right now."

She was gone before I could even protest. I was so relieved I could have dyed my own hair with Kool-Aid.

I was so happy to have the rose *and* my new

duds. I walked to my locker with the theme from *Star Wars* in my head. *Dun, **dun**, da-da-da dun* dun, da-da-da-dun-dun . . . You get the picture. I was prettier than Princess Leia. More powerful, too. I held my head high. The stares of disbelief all around me were feeding my pride, instead of killing it like they usually did.

By the way, I was wearing a too-cute jean skirt and a cropped flowered top. I even had on soft pinkish makeup. There wasn't a thread of black on my body. I did feel a little, well, naked without my dark wardrobe. But I also felt fancy and pretty — so I made myself focus on that. The more I thought about the hundreds of pep talks Genny had given me, the more I felt like a princess. Maybe it was the barrettes.

I was so full of cool confidence. People's mouths dropped open when they laid eyes on me. I took advantage and worked the drama — I grabbed my books, slammed my locker shut, and walked — make that *strutted* — to health class.

***Dun**, dun*, da-da-da **dun** dun, da-da-da-dun-dun . . .

I swear I heard a guy's voice say, "Wow, she's smokin'," as I passed.

I had no trouble ignoring the stares and whispers that day. I truly didn't care. I was going to be megapopular, even if I was the only one who thought so. I mean, the tide had turned — things were going my way for once.

I made it my mission to learn how to do Genny's magic spell.

Then I turned my attention to Gretchen. I was excited to make my move and talk to her — I didn't feel one tad terrified. I decided to do it during third-period geometry, which we had together. Can you say boring? I had already studied isosceles triangles at my old school, so I did more yawning than formulating. That gave me more time to perfect my Gretchen plans. When the bell rang, I bolted out of my seat — she sits three desks in front of me — to ask her a question on her way out of the room.

"Gretchen," I said with a friendly smile on my face.

"Uh, yeah." She turned around. She was actually *stopping* to have a conversation with me. *The* Gretchen Taylor. She was class president, cheerleading captain, newspaper editor, Honor Society member, AYM founder, *and* lead actress in the school play. At this school, being in the play was mega cool. I really wanted to do that, too. No one could come close to her hipness in middle school. She was a flawless example of popularity blended with talent.

"I've been meaning to ask you about something," I said.

"Sure, shoot." She smiled at me.

"I would love to join the newspaper staff. Do you need volunteers?" I also would've asked her about the drama department, but that would be pushing it.

"We *always* need volunteers. My life is so crazed lately that I can use any spare pair of manicured fingernails. We have our next meeting tomorrow after school." She lifted her hand to brush her gorgeous straight hair out of her black-brown eyes. Her nails were so nicely done — I had forgotten to do that. And she was stunningly beautiful — a Halle Berry look-alike.

"I'll be there, then."

"Okay, what's your name so I can put you on the list?"

What's my name? Normally, I'd be hurt by this question, but instead I was thrilled. If Gretchen didn't know my name, then she didn't know I was the birdlike Brooklyn kid from New York. And that meant I had a fighting chance of actually becoming friends with her.

"Nadia," I said. "Nadia Newton."

"Great. By the way, you look too cute. Where did you get that outfit?" she asked. Lucky for me, she walked off before I could answer her. What was I going to say? *"Oh, my genie made it for me"?* That would definitely make her want to be friends with me, huh?

I went back to my locker, and there was the red rose. Frieda had already picked it up for me. She is an adorable person. Really, she is. It was so beautiful, even if it only cost a dollar fifty at a gas station called Chug-a-Lug's. It was the perfect ending to my perfect conversation with the star of our whole entire school.

I'm telling you, happiness is having your own genie.

I spent my next few days doing all of the things that Genny told me to do. I dressed up in one of her outfits every day — she had trillions of them ready for me. Lucky for me, my parents went to work before I got dressed. Otherwise, they'd think I had stolen, like, an entire mall! I always had to change back into my old clothes before they got home.

I don't care what anybody says, when you look good, you feel great. Believe me, I felt fabtabulous. I mean, I was dolled up better than any up-to-the-minute fashion model. But somehow, I was still dressed-down enough to be cool at my new Midwest school. I took time to smell my rose, which I had taped to the inside of my locker door, at least three times a day. And I replaced it at the first sign of wiltyness. I also stopped eating microwaved food. I had no clue why Genny wanted me to do that, but I wasn't about to question a thing she said.

I spent my time between classes making nice with the popular girls — secretly hoping I wouldn't run into Frieda and Matthew at the same time. Genny didn't tell me to do that, but I couldn't smile and act cool to Gretchen's friends if I had members of the Secret Geek Society hanging around. I also tried to keep strutting around, with good posture and a bit of 'tude. Genny told me that would send out a message of *Watch out, here comes Nadia*. I really think people got that I'm-all-that vibe from me — and they seemed to like me for it. I have no idea why this worked, but I wasn't going to complain.

I went to the newspaper meeting, where I found out that Gretchen and I really did have a lot in common. She loves poetry, too, and she even asked me to write some sappy rhymes for the Valentine issue of the paper. That was exciting in itself. I don't know if I'm any good at it, but I love to write poetry. And the fact that Gretchen asked me to do it — oh my goodness, oh my goodness!

She also asked me to write a story about the swim team. The one that Chris was on! I was pretty psyched until I found out the article was supposed to be about how great all the swimmers were, and how hard they'd worked all year. Problem was, the guys hadn't won a single meet. They were so stinky, they didn't even qualify to go to the local conference. Gretchen told me, "This piece will be challenging. See what you can do."

Oh, the pressure!

At least that conversation got me invited to sit at Gretchen's lunch table on Friday. Now, *that* was pretty exciting. Gretchen was in front of me in the salad line, so I didn't dare miss a chitty-chatty opportunity. I said, "I have a few of my poems with me if you'd like to see them sometime."

"Cool! I'd love to," she replied. "Why don't you come sit with me and let me read them!"

And that was that.

Her friends Whitney, Kysa, Shapezee, Kelly, and Christie weren't thrilled to see me there. But they were polite enough. I definitely think Kelly knew my true, hidden identity. I could tell by the way she stared at me. As long as she didn't make any chirping noises, I could handle her.

"So, Nadia," Kelly began, "where did you come from again?"

"Brooklyn, New York."

"New York? Oh, that's what I thought. . . . "

Gretchen saved me. "Yeah, and didn't you tell me you saw Madonna in a pizza joint once?"

"Yeah, I did. She was incognito, but I could

totally tell it was her — she has the most distinctive nose. She was so teeny-tiny. I mean, she was, like, my size."

Shapezee and Whitney were stunned. They thought I was cool. Kelly shot me dirty looks. I just smiled at her.

But here's the very best, most earth-shattering part: Chris and a couple of other cutie-pie guys were SITTING RIGHT ACROSS THE TABLE FROM ME! I could barely swallow my salad, I was so happy about that. For the first time, he said hello and had a real conversation with me in public. He asked me how I liked my new house — and how middle school was going so far. I lied and told him how great it had been from the very beginning. I was so happy — he was just as sweet to me as he'd been when we first met in our neighborhood.

He's the one who said to Kelly, "You should invite Nadia to your birthday party tonight."

"Yeah, that's a great idea!" Gretchen seconded.

Kelly didn't look one bit happy about that, but what was she going to do? She was forced to invite me at that point. She shot Gretchen a dirty look — right in front of me, isn't that rude? But she forced a smile my way while she reached in her purse and handed me the piece of paper. It stated: "Ring in Kelly's thirteenth birthday! It's a bash for K and her closest friends. Please be sweet and come with a special treat — for her!"

Her closest friends! Okay, so I knew that wasn't me. But if she'd give me a chance, it could be. And Gretchen already thought I was pretty cool. Chris liked me, too. My loneliness would forever be over if I went to this party. I just hoped Genny had a supercool present stashed away in that bottle of hers. I knew she'd have the perfect outfit. I wanted to majorly impress Gretchen, Chris, and even Kelly. Then it hit me harder than an overcrowded school bus: *Chris would be there!*

Kelly interrupted my thoughts, which I was thoroughly enjoying. She asked, "Aren't you friends with those Einstein losers? I mean, I thought you were like best friends with that Frieda freak."

Whitney, Shapezee, Kysa, and Christie went, "Ewww," all at once. Gretchen and Chris were just looking at me. For the first time all day, I felt a little less than cool.

"You can't invite her, you know," Kelly said.

I was quiet. My face turned rashy red, and I didn't have a clue what to say. I knew Frieda wouldn't be sitting far away, so I didn't dare open my mouth.

"Listen, don't even *think* about bringing her

to my party. You won't, right?" Kelly asked.

"Right?" she asked again.

"Uh, yeah. Right," I said.

"That's right, it's my party."

Ugh. I had never said anything against Frieda out loud — just mentally, and even then, only once or twice. My whole body tingled I felt so bad about it. The only thing that eased my mind was she probably didn't hear a thing that had been said. And she'd never have to find out about it. Then, to my horror, I saw her out of the corner of my eye. She had been sitting right behind me. She got up from the table and ran out of the cafeteria. She *had* to have heard me. I felt so low, but it's not like I could show it and still be cool.

So I pretended that nothing had happened. I must have been a pretty good actress, because the girls saw the whole scene and seemed pleased that I didn't let on that I cared. Christie was just like, "Yeah, well, that's good. I don't think I could handle being friends with someone who's friends with a total dweeb."

Gretchen started talking about the upcoming school play tryouts. She was last year's lead — *and* president of drama club. That sounded *so* cool — I hoped I'd be invited to try for a part — things were definitely going in the right direction. Then my mind went back into Frieda mode. I couldn't touch my salad. I was too upset about the damage I had just done to Frieda's feelings. I thought of the rose she had rushed out to get me.

"Nadia, do you need a ride to the party tonight?" Gretchen asked, bringing me back to the cool lunch table. "Maybe we could go together."

"Well, I practically live next door to her — maybe we should go," Chris replied, turning bright red, his freckles disappearing underneath his blush. The other girls stared at him like they were surprised by what he'd said.

At first I didn't think I'd heard him right. Could Gretchen and Chris really be one-upping each other to see who gets to show up with *me*? I tell you, this was wacky.

"I would like to go with you both!" I said.

"Gretchen, you're going with me. We already had plans," Shapezee interrupted.

"Oh, yeah," she answered. "Well, Chris, I guess you get Nadia all to yourself."

He smiled at me shyly and sweetly, then said, "My mom and I will pick you up at seven."

"Okay," I said, smiling this so-stupid, goofy grin.

Ahhh . . . I was happier than Genny with a handful of pepperoni. Life would be perfect except for that terrible Frieda flub. I had a genie who obeyed my every command; Gretchen actually liked me; I was invited to a member of the cool clique's party; and Chris was taking me there with him!

Chirp-chirp Brooklyn from New York? Who's she? She's history!

The boys who had taped feathers to my back less than a week ago were staring at me. *Ha-ha, look who I'm sitting with*, I said to them with my eyes. I smiled my fakest grin at them. When I was sure no one at my cool table was looking, I stuck my tongue out at the tall one.

Chapter 10
"Oh, I Want to Do a Million Things"
by Genny the Genie

I woke up all confused—just wondering where the heck I was. I had been dreaming about my long-lost love with Frederick all darned night. Oh, how I missed him! We were such good friends!

It didn't help that I also kept dreaming about that silly spell trick I pulled on Nadia. I am not supposed to do things like that. After all, I wasn't being totally truthful like genies are supposed to be. I had to remind myself that I did it for a reason. And so what? After a thousand years, what are they going to do? Fire me?

I don't think so.

I try to be the best genie in the whole world. I have received numerous awards, more than any other genie on Earth. There was one great genie before me. She was known as the First

Genie. But something terrible and unspeakable happened to her. Right before I was appointed the Year 1000 Genie, she gave up her life of do-gooding. She relinquished her geniehood to become a mortal once again. I heard the pressure and loneliness of the years had taken their toll on her. We genies don't have real friends, we are forbidden to fall in love, and, well, we can crack just like anybody else! She must've cracked. After being a nun's genie, she became a nun, too. She died in a monastery the same day her nun friend died.

If I was going to give up my genie-hood — and believe me, I've been tempted a few times — I think it would be for true love. It's a good thing I met my Frederick *before* I technically became a genie. But that's how I am, a sappy ancient sistah.

There are so many times I wish I could have met the First Genie. I have had hundreds of questions in my lifetime — and she's the only one who could have answered them. She knows what it's like to be me.

Now I've survived even longer than she did. The milestone really made me sad. You know how turning thirty freaks humans out? That's what it was like for me. One thousand years — I really can't believe it. I feel like a thirteen-(million)-year-old fossil sometimes. Despite my modern outlook on life, love, and the pursuit of chattiness — I love Madonna, for example, and I don't mean the biblical one — I am ancient. I am literally ancient. I would be worth a lot of money if I were an artifact.

I am world-renowned — in my remote world, that is. We genies rarely meet, only once or twice in all eternity, but we do keep in touch over genie-mail. And those humans think e-mailing one another is a nineties concept! Anyway, that's how I heard about a new great genie — the Year 2000 Genie — who's being compared to me. I can't help it — I'm jealous. Not that I should feel threatened. I've lived a long life and improved the state of the world, one human being at a time. But I hear this girl has a few of the same gifts I do. . . .

That makes me feel not so special, I'm afraid. I don't think I like her. Wait a minute, I *know* I don't like her.

So I understand what people like Nadia go through. I am not perfect. I have human feelings. I know what it's like to be insecure and scared. That's Nadia's biggest problem. If she'd just be her cool self, she'd be popular. I know it. But that's why I'm here, to help her find that beautiful person who's in there somewhere.

Really, helping Nadia has been fun. After all, I've been called to help thirteen-year-olds with complicated matters like ghost-chasing and famine before. I'm thanking my Throttle that this one's such a blast! Nadia makes it a snap, too. She wakes up bright-eyed and bushy-haired every morning, just ready for the next school adventure. She hops out of bed all excited to put on whatever awesome outfit I've whipped up. I'm a trollop when it comes to getting compliments, and she gives me oodles on my clothing. I think this arrangement is working out nicely.

I was particularly inspired this morning — maybe it was the light in Nadia's eyes or the gleam on her teeth. (I envy her pearly choppers; we didn't exactly have Colgate in the year 1000.) After she left, I turned on her stereo and boogied with Catfish to my favorite music.

I had some time on my hands. Just for the record, I'd like to say that I love lounging in teens' bedrooms. They're so cozy and comfy and climate-controlled. It sure beats trying to amuse myself in a one-room hut or a mouse-infested barn like I did in the old days. I bet Catfish misses the mice — but hey, we have pepperoni now!

I sat on Nadia's tie-dyed bedspread, got out my knitting kit, and made a sweater. Next, I read a schoolbook called *History Makes People Happy*. It was so inaccurate! It said very little was known about Christopher Columbus's childhood — well, why didn't they just ask me? He was such a cool dude! All of that took me about an hour.

Then I had a good idea. I decided to go on a mission. An exciting one, too: I was going boy-snooping! Lately Nadia was way too busy to get me the dish I needed on her dude, Chris. So I decided to do the romance research myself. If I was going to help Nadia nab this guy's heart, there were things I needed to know! Like what kind of music does he dance to? Who's his bestest buddy? What's his favorite TV show? And what color are the socks he wears? After a pep talk, my kitty and I made plans to get the scoop. Catfish was *not* happy about this. He hissed and bit when I told him we were leaving the bedroom. He'd much rather dance around or lie on the bed all day instead of actually working. Cats. I swear.

Before I went anywhere, I had to take human form. Now *that* is a naughty, naughty, strictly forbidden thing. But I decided that I was tired of missing life. Just because I'm a genie doesn't mean I shouldn't be able to *really* live some-times. I had been cooped up in Nadia's room for a week. And I was sick of sitting around while she got to go out and have all of the fun.

I wiggled my nose three times, shook my hips

for two straight minutes, then rubbed my left earlobe. That's the secret formula for becoming human.

Voilà!

It worked! And goodness, it felt great. I hadn't been human for hundreds of years. I pulled my hair and felt pain. I rubbed my eyes because they itched. I took a big deep breath and smelled the breakfast everyone ate that morning. Oh, my . . . and I was hungry.

The first thing I did was change out of my lazy-day genie clothes into one of the awesome outfits I'd made for Nadia. I modeled in the mirror and pranced around the room. Sure, I'm cute and all when I'm a genie — but when I'm human, I can feel pretty from my head hairs to my tippy-toes in a way that's much more real. It's like when you come back from the beauty salon with a perfect, can't-be-duplicated 'do. You feel beautiful.

Luckily no one else was home — otherwise they would have seen me. I went down to the kitchen to get some grub. When I'm human, I'm *so* hungry. I even tried some of Nadia's health food. Lucky for me, Pizza Tofu Munchies aren't as bad as they sound. I went back up to my room to round up the cat. He was acting as bad as I'd expected him to. Not only did he want to sleep, he also was mad at me for breaking the rules. He's always afraid that I'll be forced into retirement if I make the genie council too mad. I tried to calm him down by petting him, but he still couldn't relax. I gave that bag of whiskers' tail a nice yank to convince him to scat out the door. Not even he could ruin my mood.

After all, I was human!

Chapter 11
"Way Too Many Discoveries"
by Genny the Genie

So we left for our journey to Chris's house — two doors down the street.

No one was home, so Catfish did his trick. (Only because I threatened to hog all of our pizza later!) He slipped through the pet door and let me in. When I'm not in human form, Nadia is the only one who can see me. (Usually two specially chosen friends can, too, but Nadia hadn't chosen to share her secret with anybody.) When I'm a person, I have to be careful just like you do if you ever go on a snooping spree.

I crept through the hallway until I found what had to be a boy's room. He had an old Snoopy fishing pole sitting next to a nice, new, adult-sized one. There were baseball cards lying all around.

What struck me first was that the room

seemed like a lonely place. There were empty photo albums on his desktop. Plus, he had pictures around his dresser mirror, but none of them were of people — just things. I got the feeling that he must be a little sad himself. He had a few certificates for doing well in school, and every birthday card his mother had ever given him, but there was no sign of a best friend. It just goes to show you that everyone is lonely in his or her own way.

He'd left a big stack of printed-out pages next to his computer. I glanced at them, thinking they were school papers or something. But what I found was much juicier than that. It was a journal. He must've kept it on his computer, and for some reason, he had printed it out. I know it was bad for me to look — I know! I know! I couldn't help myself, though. It was sitting there staring at me so I took a quick glimpse. . . .

What I found out surprised me beyond belief. He said he was painfully shy. And he wrote that he didn't even think he was popular like Nadia had said he was. Instead, he's a dopey dork. He isn't sure that any of his friends genuinely like him. He isn't comfortable sitting with that cliquey group of girls and guys every day at lunch — he just stays there because he doesn't know anyone else at school. Apparently, he

went to kindergarten with the whole crowd —
and he's been unhappy with the things they say
and do ever since. To put it the way Chris does,
Kelly's a "spoiled brat"; Kysa can be "cruel";
Whitney "does whatever they say"; and
Shapezee is a "bleep." He wrote that Gretchen
is genuinely sweet, and she's the only one he
really likes. He says she's brilliant and nonshal-
low, and she has been since they were babies.
He knows because their moms are friends. He
did call her "self-absorbed," but that's much
better than what he called everyone else.

Ugh! If I took Chris's word for it, Nadia
wanted to be friends with a not-so-great group.
But I wasn't going to tell her about any of this
yet. I wanted her to come to her own conclusions. People don't listen when you come to
conclusions for them.

Anyway, Chris doesn't really have guy pals,
either. He said the ones on the swim team
should have "No Diving" signs posted on their
foreheads because they are so shallow. How
awful! He just hangs with them because he's
known them since they swam in the tadpole
league.

Chris's biggest wish in life is to make some
real friends — he thinks he's too quiet, and no
one will like him. He wrote that he took a huge
chance when he went over to "the new girl's"

house to say hello. That's Nadia! She's not gonna believe this! He was so terrified to do it — but determined for once in his life to try. It turns out that he really liked Nadia. He thought she was different and cool.

So why did he stop talking to her at school? I wonder. But it doesn't sound like he talks to anyone much during the day.

When he's not swimming, he likes to take pictures with his thirty-five-millimeter cameras. He keeps this passion of his private — he's always afraid that the cool kids will rip on him for carrying a camera around his neck. So he snaps shots like crazy on the weekends when no one is around. His walls are covered with pictures of beautiful flowers and bumblebees. He likes to shoot statues and buildings, too. He even has his own darkroom, where he taught himself how to develop film. He posts his best pics up on the Internet anonymously, so someone besides his family can tell him they're wonderful.

"Oh, oh, oh! Catfish, did you find his Web site?" I asked. He had been looking for good mouse-hunting sites while I was doing my reading.

He wagged his tail yes.

And even better, he got Chris's e-mail address: tadpole13@sweetdude.com.

Now we're cookin'!

"Great work, Catfish. Give me a paw!"

We looked at the clock — we'd been there for two hours. So we decided we'd better split. We snuck through the house, and thankfully no one had come home. I was nervous about getting caught. If I got thrown in the slammer for breaking in or something, I'd go down in genie history as an outlaw. Oh, goodness, that would be a first. I breathed a huge, deep sigh of relief when I was out on the sidewalk.

Then it happened. The worst — or best? — thing I've seen in one thousand years.

Stunned silly would be putting my feelings mildly. Walking up the lane was — I swear on Throttle I'm not lying — walking up that lane was Frederick.

I stared and stared and stared some more. The cute dude looked at me just as intently. Had my one true soul mate come back to life? I had no idea if I even believed in reincarnation. But at that moment, I wanted to.

It was so hard keeping my head on straight. The eyes, the hair, the gently boyish smile . . . The way he walked — kinda cute and clumsy . . . Everything about him was the same as the long-lost love of my endless life. Frederick was the guy I was all set to marry before I became a genie.

Oh, my mind flashed to those wonderful, lazy days we spent together. We'd have picnics by the pond and do our daily chores while we kept each other company. We would steal kisses and long embraces when we knew the adults weren't watching. Sure, we were young — but we were true kindred spirits. When you find true love, you hold on to it. That's what we did. He was the best friend I ever had. I had to leave Frederick without saying good-bye — it's been a millennium, and I'm still not over it. I loved him with all my heart. And I always will.

He was the boy of my dreams. He was the meaning in my life.

I held back my tears as the boy walked closer and closer to me. I had stopped right where I was, in front of the house I had been snooping in. This boy stopped right there, too.

I tightened my ponytail so it would sit higher on top of my head. My hair draped around my face and shoulders. I felt so pretty. I smiled, and he smiled back. His expression was sweet and soulful, exactly like Frederick's would have been. I reached out for this boy's hand and said hello.

"Hi," he said quietly. He stared into my eyes with amazement. Was it *him*? Was I going crazy? I am sure I was losing my cool. He was, too. He turned beet-red.

"I saw you walking down the street. I didn't mean to stare," I said, looking away. "But I just had to say hello."

He replied, "It's nice to meet you, too." He was obviously very shy and nervous.

"You, too."

"You're beautiful," he said to me, then put his head down. I think he was embarrassed and surprised by what he'd said. "Have I met you somewhere before?"

"I don't know. I'm thinking so."

"Do you go to school with me?"

"I, um, yeah. I guess. I do." Well, I kinda did, through Nadia. The looks we were giving each other said more than any words. We had that instant connection — something just clicked. It was a meaningful moment. Sometimes you don't have to speak, and you already feel like you know everything.

Then I saw *her,* and the moment was put on hold. Nadia was coming from the other direction. She was far away, but I didn't have much time. I didn't want her to spot me on the street and find out what I had been up to!

"I'm sorry," I said as I rushed away from the greatest guy of all my dreams.

He yelled, "Wait! Please wait. At least tell me your name!"

It's Genevieve, I wanted to say, but didn't.

That's what people called me in France. I missed hearing the word. Maybe if this guy *was* my Frederick, that name would have rung a bell.

I ran around the block so Chris wouldn't see me slip into Nadia's house, beating her by about a minute. As I walked in the back door, I saw the mysterious boy walk into the house I'd just been investigating.

Oh, my worst black plague.

He was Nadia's Chris — and maybe my Frederick, too.

Chapter 12
"My Genie Is Malfunctioning"
by Nadia

After the day I'd had, I was dying to talk to Genny. Bursting, actually. But as soon as I got home from school, I heard a snoring noise from inside of Throttle. What the heck was that? Since when do genies sleep at three in the afternoon on a Friday?

I decided to give her an hour — if I could wait that long to talk to her, that is. . . . I definitely needed some help for this party!

I NEED MY GENIE!

Chapter 13
"I Think I Can, I Think I Can – I Can't"
by Genny the Genie

I had hit play on my snore machine. After what I had just been through, there was no way I could face Nadia until I got myself together. I went back into genie form and hid inside Throttle, trying desperately to figure out how to deal with this terribly sticky situation.

First on my mind was my Frederick. Oh, how I missed him! I missed being loved and loving someone. I missed having a life. When you're human, you're capable of feeling these warm and fuzzy things. And I was feeling them so much more intensely than I had in centuries. Oh, it hurt to love — but it was wonderful at the same time. These feelings made me question why I was a genie in the first place. Why make everyone else happy when I'm not always happy? I wanted to feel this way forever.

I knew I had been very bad. Obviously, there are reasons genies aren't supposed to take human form. It's a condition that makes us want what we can't have. I started to feel guilty about questioning my geniehood. Being a genie is a huge honor. And I've helped so many people out of their pickles. The world may not have seen great people like Abe Lincoln or Christopher Columbus if I had never become what I am today.

The thoughts overcame my brain. I cried and cried. That's another thing genies don't often do.

And then I freaked. WHAT IF CHRIS WAS FREDERICK? And there I was, given the assignment to set him up with someone else. Fate is not known for being fair, and in this instance, I had cold, hard, hurtful proof. The bottom line, no matter how much it hurt me, was to help Nadia. If I was going to continue to be a genie, that's what I had to do. I would have to put my feelings aside. But with the throbbing and emptiness in my head and my heart, I didn't know if it would be possible. I was scared. I had never hated my geniehood like I did at that very moment.

I wasn't only a bad genie who broke every rule possible. I was also a heartbroken genie.

I could hear Nadia bouncing around all

happy and giggly over something, so I had to think fast. I knew she'd rub Throttle and demand my help any minute. I couldn't throw a thousand years away in five minutes, so I decided to forget about the whole thing. At least for now. I would try to forget Frederick and Chris. I swore to myself I would try.

Sure enough, Nadia rubbed. Whether I liked it or not — *poof*! I was out of the bottle. I tried to be slick and not let on about anything that had just happened. It was actually easy because Nadia was in a real tizzy and not tuned in to me (thankfully). Her barrettes were all crooked in her messed-up hair. She had the biggest grin ever. I thought her ears would crack in half! At least one of us was sincerely happy. I was just faking it at that moment.

"What happened, *ma amie*? Do tell! Do tell!" I made myself jump up and down and dance around. I had to pretend — I just didn't want her to suspect that anything was weird with me. Meanwhile, Nadia hugged me and hugged me and hugged me some more. At least her happy mood was kinda contagious. Then she spilled the secret — she had been invited to Kelly's birthday party.

Kelly? I thought. *Uh-oh.* I grimaced, but she didn't notice. I didn't want to let it slip that I had been snooping in Chris's house. I didn't want to tell her that I wasn't so sure about this girl named Kelly.

"And guess who I'm going with? Chris!"

Ever had a sword poked through your heart? Me neither, but I knew what it would feel like as soon as she spoke those words. *With Chris? My Chris? My Frederick?* I told myself, *I will forget about them. I will be a good genie. I will forget Chris and Frederick forever. I will. I will. I will.*

Catfish hissed in Nadia's direction. He was upset for me.

"What's wrong?" Nadia asked.

"Nothing. Catfish just had something in his eye," I replied. "So, go on, go on!" I tried to sound authentically excited. "Tell me everything!"

She spilled out the entire story of her day, from her chitchat with Gretchen in the lunch line to being invited to the party with Chris. I listened with patience — that's one thing I've learned a lot about after one thousand years. When her excitement slightly subsided, I changed the subject. I asked, "Do you think those girls are nice?"

She answered, "I think Gretchen's great! But I have to get to know the others before I make judgments about them."

After everyone had judged *her* so fast — and made her so sad — I thought that Nadia's statement showed her true, inner sugariness.

"But why do you want to be friends with popular kids?" I had to ask.

"They get the best of everything, that's all. And I want people to think so highly of me, too."

"What if they're not such great people?"

"Genny, what's going on with you?"

The last thing I wanted to do was burst her happy bubble, so I decided to drop Chris's disses for now. Anyway, what if he was wrong? Besides, I had the real scoop on her dude, and we had stuff to do. I told Nadia all about Catfish's gift for sussing out secrets and breaking into kids' bedrooms. My kitty modeled about the room, acting like it was all true. I was thankful the furball was covering for me — and our day's activities. I told Nadia that Chris was truly shy.

I paused while I said to myself, *Forget Chris. Forget Frederick.*

"Nadia, he's probably a great guy." It killed me to say that. "And best of all," I went on, "he wrote that you are cool!" The sword was going deeper and deeper into my heart.

She jumped up and down again.

"If you're going to woo him, I want you to start wooing him via genie-mail."

"Huh?" Nadia said.

"Oh, I mean e-mail."

With that, we went Web surfin'. More for me than for her, we looked up Chris's photographs — and both of us were way impressed. We printed out some pictures he'd taken of birds and gave them to Catfish. I kept a picture he had taken of a daisy for myself. Then we got down to business.

"Type this," I said. " 'Hi! I love you! I love everything about you. I'm forever yours, my honeydew. Love, Nadia.' " She thought I was kidding, but truth was, that's what *I* wanted to tell him.

She wrote that sentence with hearts and loopy letters on a piece of paper, laughing. Then she wadded it in a ball and threw it on the floor. "I can't send him something like that! Where did you get honeydew?!"

"Oh, never mind," I said. "Okay, so type this: 'Hi, tadpole13@sweetdude.com. I love your photos. I bet you get compliments like that all of the time. I'm a little shy, but I saw your pics and have to say I admire you. I am thirteen and live in the Midwest. What about you? I would be so excited if you wrote me back.' "

Just as we were finishing up, Nadia heard a knock at the door and peeked out the window.

"Oh, no! Hide fast! It's my cousin Frieda and her friend Matthew. Oh, no, not them! Not now!" Nadia seemed a little distressed. I wondered if she'd told me *everything* about her day.

Even though I knew Frieda and Matthew wouldn't be able to see us (since I was back in genie form), I also knew that it would distract Nadia to have us in sight. So I hid under the bed with Catfish — we wanted to make sure we could see what was about to happen. I stared like crazy when Frieda and Matthew walked in. The girl had the weirdest-colored hair, and her guy friend had a spiky 'do with way too much gel in it. Whoa — these two were definitely unique.

"We need to talk to you," Matthew said to Nadia. On second look, he was cute. Well, in a nerdy kind of way. "You really hurt Frieda's feelings today in the cafeteria. And we don't think it was right."

"We invited you into the Secret Geek Society and everything!" Frieda said as she started crying. "I tried to make you welcome. I even invited you into the Einsteins. I just tried to be nice to you. I wanted to make things easier for you."

Nadia didn't put her head up once. If she'd had a tail, it would've been between her legs. *What on earth did she do?* I wondered.

She was so excited a minute ago; now she looked like big-time down in the dumps.

"You know, you can hang out with the cool kids and still like us, too," Matthew said. "I mean, hang out with them if you prefer *them*." He sounded very wounded.

"It's not that I don't like you two . . . uh," Nadia muttered. "I don't, like, prefer them or anything."

"I'm convinced, how about you, Matthew?" Frieda asked sarcastically, and he shrugged his shoulders, wanting to give Nadia the benefit of the doubt.

"You actually like people who are in AYM?" Frieda asked.

"I guess I do. Look, Gretchen's really nice if you give her a chance."

"Not to me she isn't."

"I wish I knew what to say! I feel awful!" Nadia said, head still hanging low.

"Sorry would be a start."

"Oh, Frieda, I'm sorry. What I said today was a mistake. I won't do anything like that ever again. I'm just going through a lot of stuff right now."

"Are you that embarrassed by me?" Frieda asked as she scooted her cut-up sweatshirt back over her shoulder. "Look, Nadia, I know the truth. I know I'm not cool."

"Of course not — of course you are," Nadia said, knowing it was probably coming out all wrong. She didn't look like her sincere self, but she still went over and hugged Frieda. Frieda just stood there, not hugging her back for a few seconds.

Matthew did the same thing, only he was obviously waiting for his hug. Just then, Catfish tried to reach out for that crumpled-up piece of paper on the ground. I knew he was bored and wanted to bat it around, so I reached out and grabbed it for him.

He lifted his paw, looked at me mischievously, and batted it straight into a backpack — the one that Matthew picked up when he and Frieda finally left Nadia's room.

He licked his chops in triumph. He was quite pleased with his practical joke.

I could have pulled out his toenails. That darn cat is always causing trouble just to cause trouble.

Didn't we have enough to deal with?

Chapter 14
"He Loves Me, He Loves Me Not . . ."
by Nadia

I don't know what everyone's problem is. It's not like I'm *not* Nadia. I'm still the same old me, only new and improved! I think Frieda and Matthew need to give me a break. They need to relax.

It even seemed like Genny wasn't thrilled with me after that scene in my bedroom. She was silent — and she's never silent. I know how I hurt Frieda's feelings. But how could I have hurt Genny's?

Genny finally let it go and got to the job at hand, which was getting me ready for my big date with Chris. She rooted through Throttle and found a cute pink sparkly sweater that I could give to Kelly as her present. I heard her humming "Somewhere Over the Rainbow" while I waited what seemed like forever for her to come out. She wasn't her peppy, chatty self — that was for sure. Usually she'd be rapping the latest tunes or something. Maybe she was deep in thought over how to help me out.

Anyway, I figured that when I gave Kelly the sweater, she'd be really glad she invited me. And everyone would think I spent *sooo* much moola! Ha! Good! If they only knew.

I dolled myself up in more of Genny's custom-made clothes and waited on the front step for Chris and his mom. My heart went into automatic overdrive when they pulled into the driveway. He was so cute! I hopped into the backseat of their minivan, and Chris barely made a peep. He was so shy, just like Genny said! His mom talked the whole time, which moms are really good at.

She asked me, "There was a girl hanging out in front of our house today before school got out. I saw her as I was leaving. Do either of you know who she was? Is she a friend of yours, Nadia?"

All I could think of was Frieda, but she would've been in school, and she definitely wouldn't have been hanging in front of Chris's house. "I don't think so."

"I didn't see any girl, Mom," Chris said, squirming. His shyness was so cute!

Finally, we arrived at Kelly's house.

Now, I expected her to have tons of money and live in a white colonial house with six bedrooms, three bathrooms, and three thousand square feet of yard. Boy, was I right. Her house looked just like mine, but much bigger. It was painted bright yellow, and the shingles on the porch looked like they were gold-plated. I've heard her say that her parents already have a new Beetle on layaway for her for when she turns sixteen. I have to say, I believe it. They even had two dishwashers.

When we got inside, it was very pink. Pink hanging balls of tissue paper; pink tinsel draped all over the light fixtures; pink plates of cupcakes with *Kelly* written on them in red; pink drinks in plastic cups that said — what else? — *Kelly*! At least my present would match her decorations. Banners with her name on it were all over the house, and I wasn't sure they were there just because it was her birthday. In the basement, where the party was, a table-sized, heart-shaped cake read, KELLY IS THE QUEEN. I didn't know whether to be in awe of a thirteen-year-old who got this much attention, or intimidated. I guess I was both.

After we got into the basement, Chris was quiet. He rolled his eyes at Kelly's indulgence.

Everyone was standing around the birthday girl telling her how great her up 'do and makeup job looked. She was going, "Thanks, thanks. MOM, can you PLEASE get me ANOTHER CUP OF LEMONADE?!! LIKE, NOW!!!"

Chris went off to talk to Gretchen, and I stood there by myself while Christie, Whitney, Kysa, and Shapezee ignored me. I was surprised that he'd leave me there like that. But it didn't take him long to come back.

My sweet, thoughtful dream guy said, "Sorry about that," and led me over to Gretchen. I was so excited — it felt like he was showing everyone that we were together. But I guess he wasn't — he and Gretchen just resumed their conversation when I got there. I wish I hadn't heard it.

He was going on and on about the amazing, beautiful, mysterious girl he had met in front of his house after school that day. Gretchen was wide-eyed and very interested. I was so disappointed. How could he possibly like another girl? I thought he was starting to like me!

Not able to hide my utter defeat, I said, "I thought you told your mom you hadn't met a girl outside your house today."

"I just said that." He smiled and went back

to his who's-that-girl discussion. He said to Gretchen, "I have never, ever in my life met a girl like this one. She was something special. I have to find her."

I walked away. I couldn't take it another second. Finally, Gretchen came over and grabbed my arm.

"Nadia! The East Coast cutie!" she said. She must have been able to tell something was wrong, but she didn't ask. I was so glad — Chris was right behind us, so I couldn't tell her anything anyway.

She whispered, "Isn't Kelly a spoiled brat?" Even though I felt birdlike, she managed to make me smile. Gretchen was cool. Next, she took me over to the crowd of girls. They finally said hi and were nice to me. I wanted them to like me — well, everyone but Kelly, maybe. I'd have to ask Genny what to do because I was clueless. I was clueless about Chris, too.

Still, I smiled and said, "Happy birthday, Kelly." She just gave me a cheesy fake grin and turned around. *Meow!* Shapezee told me how much she liked my outfit, and how much better I'd been looking lately. Kindly, Kysa didn't say anything to make me uncomfortable. And Whitney just said uh-huh and yeah to everything I said about my CD collection. I'm not sure she was even listening. Gretchen chimed in to talk about cheerleading, and everyone got all excited.

"I want to be on top of our pyramid next week," Kelly said.

"Sure thing — it's your birthday week, after all," Gretchen replied.

Then Gretchen talked about drama club and got so excited. She really seemed to love it — and the other girls loved hearing her go on about it. She told me I'd really like it, too, and I should try out soon. Then she and I got into a great conversation about the newspaper, and how we wanted to take a schoolwide vote on the "Most Likely To . . ." section this year. We yapped and yapped while everyone else got into their own discussions about boys and skirts and shoes. At least one part of the night was going okay.

We played the usual piñata games and ate cake. Kelly opened her presents — and totally loved mine, by the way. Then we danced to poppy techno music and country tunes — well, I had to be careful and not move too much. I dance too Brooklyn for this crowd and was afraid of looking like a freak. If you ask me, these Midwestern kids were having a hard time finding their groove, the guys especially. All of them except for Chris boogied like frogs in a blender.

Chris was boogying with me some. That got me back in a good mood. And my goose bumps nearly poked holes through my shirt when he asked me to come get a Coke with him. He touched my elbow and said, "You live near me. . . . Um, well, could you please help me find that girl?"

What a bummer.

Whoever she was, I hated her.

Chapter 15
"The Truth Hurts"
by Genny the Genie

She came home that night and sobbed into her pillow.

I nearly died when she wailed, "He likes another girl! Genny, what can I do? He's madly in love with her. He talked about her all night long!"

I stroked her hair and told her she was wonderful. We'd make sure he saw that soon. I comforted her like a good genie. Then her new friend Gretchen called to ask her what was really wrong. So Nadia spilled the whole story all over again. And finally she fell into a weeping, fitful sleep.

I was still awake. I couldn't begin to rest with the mess I was in.

First of all, I was torn up because I was being a bad genie. I was the kind of genie who, if I was still in my first hundred years, would be fired. (Now everyone trusts me, so my actions don't get watched that closely anymore.)

Second, I was in love with my client's most-wanted boy.

Third, I had met him and it turned out that *he* loved *me*.

Fourth — and worst of all — I knew what was right. If I had no conscience, maybe I could have been happy. But I had a conscience, and I knew exactly what it wanted me to do. I had to fix the game so Nadia would win this one.

Those were the rules of being a genie.

I had a fifth problem, too — if this was what I had to go through, I was not sure I wanted to be a genie anymore.

I had to do something about all of this, for better or for worse. So I did it — I made a decision. I was going back into human form. And, most important, I was going to find Chris. I had to know for sure if he was my Frederick. Once I knew, I would figure out some solution . . . Or die trying.

The next day of school, just as classes were letting out, I started the long walk to Nadia's school. I went to a wonderful spot where I hoped to find him sitting in the grass. That's where Catfish had spotted him on one of his legitimate outings. I waited there. And just like a dream come true, he showed up. I smiled at him as he walked my way.

"You!" he said. He looked more like my long-lost love that day than he did the day before.

"You."

We didn't know what to say to each other. But there seemed to be a deep, unspoken something between us. I asked him to walk in the nearby woods with me — I wanted to talk to him. I needed to talk to him to find the answers to my questions. I hoped — and I didn't hope — that it would really be *him*.

Nadia was right, he was so cute when he was nervous. He started off our walk by talking about the weather. The way he spoke about the sunny day made me yearn to smooch him. Oh, it's been too long since I've been kissed.

"Tell me what your life is like," I said to him. "I just moved here from far away."

"Oh, things are so boring here. There's nothing much to tell."

"Tell me about yourself."

"Well, I've lived here my whole life. I am thirteen years old, and I'm in the seventh grade. Are you a sixth grader?"

"Uh, yeah." *Sure, why not?* I thought. I had to get to some juicy stuff, or I'd never know if he was the reincarnation of my sweet French baboo. "Would you say you're happy?"

"That's a strange question to ask," he said.

"You seem different than other boys, that's all."

"I am different. I care about things that are meaningful. Kids here just care about clothes and cliques and gossip. I wish I could find a friend who isn't shallow. I like to talk about movies and music. I don't care who likes who. I think being smart and having real friends is so much more important."

Well, he was mild-mannered and supersensitive, just like my old boyfriend. I wanted to fall for this boyish freckle-faced kid so badly. Maybe this would work; maybe it *could* work. But is that what I really wanted? It would mean that . . . that I'd have to . . . oh, I couldn't bear to think about it.

"You must have some really great friends, then."

"I don't know about that. I have a lot of old friends who I know really well. But I don't want to talk about them. You seem like a really cool girl. Since we're walking toward my house, would you like to take a walk with me?"

I said sure, my heart all tingly and fluttering. My brain told me that stolen kisses would definitely not be a good idea, even though that's what I wanted. We talked about nothing the whole way home. Chatting with him was so easy — so effortless.

"I have never met a girl like you," he said.

"No, you probably haven't." I could tell he really liked me. It was flattering, but also a bit scary.

We walked through a park and sat down on a bench. I thought it was romantic. I hoped like crazy he'd kiss me. Then I would have known for sure if he was Frederick. I have forgotten a lot of things — but never Frederick's kiss. (Hey, we're French!) Or the feeling it gave me when our lips met.

"There's something I want you to see," he said.

He reached into his book bag while I was still terribly anxious to find out the truth. He pulled out the picture of the daisy! I died inside. Frederick knew those are my favorite flowers. I thought Chris was him . . . Until the next few words came out of his mouth.

Very shyly, he said, "Would you mind if I kissed you?"

His question struck me weirdly — it threw me off guard. Then it jolted me into reality, and I knew the truth: This kid could not be Frederick. Yes, Chris was polite, and I appreciated that. But Frederick would never have asked about a smooch. He just wouldn't have! He and I were so connected that he would have read my mind. With that question, it was clear that Chris couldn't read me at all. He was sweet as potato pie, but not who I wanted him to be.

Frederick knew me better than anyone else — Chris clearly did not. But I had a strong feeling that he would have a connection like that with someone else I knew. Nadia.

Time stopped for a few seconds while I zonked out into my own world. When I came back to life, total disappointment overcame me. Just like that, he was no longer mine. He was just Nadia's Chris.

Yes, I was brokenhearted, but also relieved. If he was not my boyfriend, then maybe I would be less tempted to do such naughty things like I had been doing for the past two days. Maybe then I could forget about being human. I hoped I'd never want to be human again — it was just too painful.

"Your name is Chris, isn't it?" I asked. All of a sudden, I knew I'd have to make a mad dash out of there. The longer I stayed, the more this guy would fall for me. His eyes were getting starrier by the second! And this just wasn't right, I had finally figured that out. Oh, thank my Throttle, I had figured it out!

I had to go home, not be human, and do my genie job. This boy made me miss my Frederick, and I adored Chris for that. But I didn't love Chris for Chris. I had to leave.

"How rude of me! I didn't introduce myself! Yes, I'm Chris. How did you guess?"

"I just had a feeling. I've heard very nice things about you."

"From who?"

Before I made an excuse and booked it outta there, I said, "From a sweet, special girl named Nadia."

Chapter 16
"I Hate My Mistakes"
by Genny the Genie

I am just not doing a good job.

I'm flubbing this whole entire thing. Nadia, my favorite kid client, is starting to morph into Frankenstein's monster. You haven't seen her new I'm-popular attitude yet. I had no idea that popularity would make Nadia kinda crazy. (But in the meantime, I've created a monster, and I am not proud of that.)

I am a mess. I've created a mess. And I have messed up — big-time.

I'm going to start feeling better by fixing things.

But what if I can't fix things?

Chapter 17

"I'm Not the Only One in Love"

by Nadia

It dawned on me in gym today. I've found out that I'm really good at being popular. People want to talk to me, guys say I'm cute, and I have been invited to another cool party!

There are some downsides, too. I will say that Kelly definitely doesn't dig me. I try not to care too much. I've been hoping that when her friends start to fall for me, she will, too, eventually. So I put all of my energy into Christie, Shapezee, Kysa, and Whitney. Whenever they talk, I listen intently. Whenever they have strong opinions — and they have a lot of them — I try to agree. I just don't want to make any waves when I'm wooing them.

At least I don't have to try to be friends with Gretchen. That happened naturally. I have to say it — she's forty times cooler than those other chicks. I think it's because she's open-minded and supersmart. There's more to Gretchen's charm than all-out gorgeousness. She's just got something sparkly about her, too.

It hasn't worked yet, but I hope my rise into the social stratosphere will win me love points with Chris, too. He's still oohing and aahing over that mystery girl. Doesn't he have to lose interest eventually? I am beginning to wonder if he has a thing for Gretchen, since she's the only girl besides me he ever talks to. They discuss his crush all of the time. Maybe he's just being intriguing, and the mystery girl is really *her.*

He tells me all about Gretchen when we talk outside my house. We both just agree how cool she is!

He said, "You know, Nadia, I think you and Gretchen make really great friends."

"Why?"

"You're both, you know, not fake."

"I can't stand that stuff! Like when people only care about certain brands of clothes or who went where with who. It's so silly."

"There are so many more interesting things to talk about! That's what I mean about you and Gretchen. Your friendship isn't based on that kind of stuff."

"You're right — it isn't."

"She's just a cool chick, and I can say that because I've known her forever. You two have a lot in common."

I think that meant that Chris, in his own way, was telling me I was cool, too! Oh, my goodness! I loved long conversations with him. He and I could talk forever, even if he just thought of me as a friend.

I'm driving Genny nuts, I know it. She has made it clear that she thinks I've taken this popularity thing too far. I would like to think that she's *not* right this time, and that I'm handling my new life just fine. But after what happened this afternoon, I do have to wonder. . . .

I was having a great conversation with Kysa about skirts and hairstyles. We were in the lunchroom trying to kill time. I knew a guy was standing right behind me for a while, but I couldn't be bothered to pay attention to him. I was busy bonding.

Then Kelly rudely interrupted, "Uh, Nadia, like, why is that Einstein freak stalking you?"

I turned around and — like in a very bad nightmare — Matthew was standing right there gazing at me. I asked him if he needed anything. He said, "Yes, I need to give you this." He handed me a white carnation and a note. I was so confused — and honestly embarrassed. The whole table was giggling. I asked him what it was and he replied, "Just read it. I'll call you tonight." As soon as he left, Kelly made so much fun of me. She sarcastically said I had finally found my perfect match. I thought I would die. It didn't help that Chris was sitting there staring the whole time.

Next, Whitney made me read the note out loud. I would rather have been lying in twelve feet of snow and freezing to death than reading the note at that moment. I hesitated, so she grabbed it out of my hand and read these words: " 'Nadia, you are my soul mate. I know we are living in different worlds right now. But if you give me a chance, our life can collide. I dream of kissing you. I was so happy to find out that you feel the same way, too. I will gladly be your honeydew. Thanks for the letter. You're just like heaven. I think I love you. Love, Matthew.' "

I absolutely had to save face. Not only was my table mortified, half of the lunchroom heard the ruckus. So I stated the truth: "That boy has lost it, I have no idea what he's talking about."

Everyone went, "Yeah, right." Others were saying much meaner things, like, "Ewww! What a gooberball! He's a dork!"

The scene just got worse and worse. I had no idea what I had done to deserve this — or to bring on such a love note. Kelly ripped the note out of Whitney's hands and tore it into a million pieces. Matthew was leaving the cafeteria in shame because he had seen and heard the whole thing. While he was looking, she threw the pieces in the air going, "Wheee! Wheee!"

"I was mortified for myself and for Matthew," I told Genny when I got home. "Neither one of us needed something like that to happen."

She told me to sit down. "I think Matthew *did* think you wrote that note," she said. Then she told me the whole story about how the silly love note for Chris ended up in Matthew's bag. Ugh.

If I could have caught that evil cat, I would have wrapped its tail around its neck. But since I couldn't, I called Matthew to apologize and to try to explain. I guess it's not a surprise that he wouldn't speak to me.

I love being popular, but there sure are a lot of headaches that come along with it.

Chapter 18
"I Love You, Sweet Baboo"
by Genny the Genie

Catfish really had no idea what kind of trauma he was causing by creating such a complicated love triangle. I don't think he'll be batting notes into backpacks again anytime soon. I owe it to Nadia to fix this fast, especially since this wasn't her fault at all! I did some brainstorming, and I think I've come up with a scheme to get Matthew and Frieda together. Maybe that will help.

But first, I have to throw Chris off of my love trail and get him back onto Nadia's. Actually, I think it will be quite simple.

With Catfish's help — he's the computer wiz, not me — I created an anonymous e-mail account on Nadia's computer while she was at school. Then I got to work. I typed in the e-mail address tadpole13@sweetdude.com and wrote:

hey, chris,

your mystery girl is not who you think she is. i know because i am her. i am only in the sixth grade and not allowed to hang around with boys yet. i hope you will understand. please don't miss out on true love. you might find it with someone in your own grade. so always keep your eyes open, okay?
your friend,
g.

I hit send, relieved that I had done the right thing. And just for fun, I wrote one more message:

my sweet,
i love you more today than yesterday.
i've loved for a thousand yesterdays, and every day there was only you.
i am yours forever and ever. no matter what happens, you are always, and will always be, my one and only. even if you and I are only in my dreams.
forever with you,
your g.

I read it over and over, and the memory of Frederick made me happy. I walked away so I could grab a tissue to dry my teary eyes. I heard a *thunk* and looked over at Catfish. He was chasing a fly that had landed on the computer monitor.

"Be careful!" I yelled as he landed on the keyboard. I went over there to see if he'd messed up my beautiful e-mail — I wanted to print it out and save it before it got erased.

Catfish hadn't erased it — he'd sent it to tadpole13@sweetdude.com.

Great.

I quickly whipped up another e-mail:

chris,
please disregard previous e-mail, as i have lost my mind and don't plan on finding it again anytime soon.
g.

I am not e-mailing anyone ever again.

Chapter 19
"This Is Bizarro World"
by Nadia

You never know what's going to happen during a day. I knew this one would be tough, but I wasn't expecting it to be *disturbing*. It was *The Twilight Zone*, and I'm not kidding.

I was going about my business at school. The only thing that was way unusual was how nervous I felt: I had play tryouts at three in the afternoon. I spent the day going over my lines mentally, burning them into my brain when I should have been listening to my social studies teacher. I just couldn't be bothered, though. Being in the same play as Gretchen was the key to *finally* fitting in with all of her friends. Of course, they were all the heads of some committee — props, choir, costumes. Gretchen was the lead and president of the drama club. She had hand-chosen them all. I had to actually audition to be involved with the production, since I missed all the other sign-up deadlines.

So the girls were testing me, no doubt about it. They had been pressuring me for weeks to be involved. If I was good enough to make it, I'd be good enough to hang with them. If I didn't make it, who knows what would happen? They made it seem like I'd have to find a new seat in the lunchroom.

Gretchen was the only one who actually went out of her way to tell me it didn't matter to her if I got a good part — she'd still be friends with me. But I felt stress from her anyway. I know she meant well, but she kept going over my lines with me and giving me pointers. At least she was really helpful. Genny was, too — we spent a lot of time practicing on my bed together, laughing and eating our respective pizzas.

So the big day was there, and we were all getting ready in the girls' room. (For some reason, the director wanted us to audition in costume — he said it would help him with the "look" of the play. Whatever.) The cool girls were changing their clothes and there were only two other girls trying out for the part I was just *dying* for. I was nowhere near calm. I was preoccupied with audition perfection. And when my guard was down, the girls made their move.

Kelly, Christie, Shapezee, and Whitney

crowded around and cornered me in front of a bathroom stall. A few girls were also in the rest room, but my new friends didn't seem to care. Something was definitely up.

"I heard that girl named Frieda was your cousin, Nadia," Kelly said.

"Yeah, we all heard it," Christie added, glaring at me.

"Well, so," I replied.

"So? *Sooo?!*" Christie went on. At this point, the conversation was making me nervous. "That means you didn't tell us the truth about her."

"We were shocked," Kelly added. "Just so shocked."

"Why?" I asked, suddenly seeing them as stalking barracudas.

"Well, we can't have a loser like her bringing down our image," Kelly huffed. "You don't plan to actually *talk* to her if you get the part, do you?"

I was trying to think of something to say. This was tricky territory.

"Because, you know, we do get to vote on who gets the part — we're all committee chairs," Kelly said. "Tell her, Whitney."

Whitney stopped twirling the blue gum around her finger and added, "We'd never vote for you unless you totally deny your cousin-hood."

"Huh?" They were losing their minds.

"Prove to us that you want to be one of us," Kelly said. "Tell us she's a total dweeb, and you'd rather have a great part than ever speak to her again."

"You'll get it if you do," Shapezee said.

"You agree she's a dweeb, right?" Kelly asked.

I didn't say anything. How could I? They were putting me on the spot.

"I *knew* you'd agree," Kelly said next.

But I never uttered a word to her! Just when I was about to get mad and tell her to stop putting words in my mouth, Kelly walked over to another bathroom stall and opened the door.

To my horror, Frieda had been sitting in there listening the whole time. I looked her in the eyes — it was clear she had been crying. She bolted out the door, trying not to show any of us how upset I knew she really was.

"The part is yours," Kelly said.

"You're sick," I replied.

"I just wanted to make sure you wouldn't go back on your word," Kelly coldly explained. "This can be confusing. I want it to be as clear as possible. So I waited until I saw her come in here. She deserves it, that Secret Geek Society loser."

The three girls giggled. I was stunned. I had no idea that cruel things like this actually happened anywhere but on bad TV shows. And I had been a part of it all. I was so shocked that I became completely catatonic for at least five seconds.

They started hugging me and laughing. I couldn't even smile over the thought that I had gotten what I really wanted — the part. I was just plain horrified. I left the bathroom, tears streaming down my cheeks.

Is this what I was dying to be a part of?

Chapter 20
"I Am Mean"
by Nadia

I think I did the right thing. I ran out of the girls' room to look for Frieda. I had to try to comfort her. At that moment, I would have done anything to take back the last five minutes. I knew how hurt she must have been feeling. I noticed that Kysa was standing outside the rest room, and she must have heard everything. She looked as unhappy as I did.

She pointed me in the direction she had seen Frieda running. I went. I knew I would never get the part, because I was missing the auditions. But I cared a little less for every minute that I couldn't find my cousin.

I never found her. I even called her house from a pay phone at school. She wasn't there. So then I called Matthew's — that's how bad I wanted to talk to her.

"Hello," he said.

"Matthew, this is Nadia."

"Nadia who?" he said, obviously peeved at me. "What the heck is going on? First you humiliate me. Now you want to pass around some fake picture of us together just to make Frieda quit. That's what Kelly told me you did. You're a horrible person. I can't believe I actually did have a crush on you once."

"So you've already heard what happened. . . . "

"Yes, I know what happened. Frieda is in my bathroom bawling right now."

"Tell her I'm sorry."

"Can't you just leave her alone? Can't you just leave *us* alone?"

His words hurt me, especially since I knew that was really how he felt. It dawned on me that I actually cared what Matthew and Frieda thought. I was much more worried about them than I was about anyone else.

But all I could say was, "I'm sorry for what I did to you. And I'm even sorrier for what I did to my cousin."

Chapter 21
"It's Hard to Shock Me – But I Am Shocked"
by Genny the Genie

Nadia didn't want to talk. I was all set to hear about her tryouts. My chattiness was coming back because I had started to recover from my Frederick Funk.

But instead of dancing to Madonna or playing dress-up with me, Nadia said she was tired and went straight to bed at four o'clock. I heard her weeping into her pillow before she fell asleep. I didn't dare ask her where my pepperoni pizza was.

I had to pull a few genie strings to find out what on earth had gone wrong. It didn't take a genie-ous to see that whatever it was, it was bad.

Catfish hissed and had a fit when I sent him over to the school. I told him I'd have a Q-Tip waiting if he'd do a good job with this assign-

ment. I also had to promise him a night off —
he wanted to go alley-catting in the neighborhood before our twenty-eight days with Nadia
were over.

I sat down beside Nadia awhile and watched
her sleep. She looked troubled, so I stroked her
hair while I waited for that darn cat. Lucky for
him, he was back within an hour to wiggle his
tail and sign me the whole sad story.

How does life get so complicated?

Apparently, after Nadia bailed, there were
two stories going around the play tryouts.
According to the so-called cool girls, Nadia had
ripped apart her cousin just to be mean and
evil. They reported to Gretchen that Nadia was
trying to get Frieda out of her life forever. Kelly
put it to Gretchen this way: "It's just too bad
Nadia had to use *us* to help her."

The other story came from the roaches in the
bathroom that witnessed the whole scene. How
Catfish got them to talk, I don't know. But they
said that Nadia hadn't even dissed on her
cousin. It was all a lie! Kelly dissed Frieda,
Nadia didn't! Nadia didn't even know that the
girls had waited until Frieda was in earshot of
their cruel conversation. It sounded like the
drama girls were peeved about the Secret Geek
Society — so they decided to use Nadia to teach
Frieda a lesson. It's hard to surprise me — I've

seen some pretty barbaric things throughout the years. But this was up there with the craftiest and cruelest of them all. These kids of the two thousands, I swear. And Nadia wanted to be friends with them?

I knew the second story Catfish told me was true, because I knew my Nadia. She wasn't one bit cruel, even if she had been making a lot of mistakes lately. Meanwhile, if I hadn't been so caught up with Frederick — I mean, Chris — maybe I could have stopped this mess.

This situation was terrible, but it wasn't as bad as another one I'd gotten myself into years ago. I was helping a thirteen-year-old named Pierre survive during the appalling craziness of the French Revolution. I was too busy trying to make sure the French Blue — you know it as the Hope Diamond, by the way — didn't get into the wrong hands. The common people who were stealing the royal jewelry didn't know how powerful and cursed that one particular piece of rock was. So I was on a mission to make sure a wizard or someone with powers would get it and protect the people from the darned thing. In the meantime, my client, who eventually turned out to be a member of the new French parliament, got separated from his family and didn't find them for ten years. It was all because I wasn't paying attention. Granted, I helped some people, but I had let my client down. I never know what is more important. I have trouble with that.

I did know this, though: I had let Nadia down, too.

That's what it's like being a genie. You can never be sure if what you are doing is right. I pretty much have to follow my masters' wishes, but it's also my job to make sure things go smoothly for everybody involved. I'm supposed to keep hurtful things from happening while I make wishes come true. But no matter what I do, I find that task impossible. I don't have the same excuse you have. I'm *not* only human. Maybe I just need more experience. Maybe I'm not as good a genie as everyone says.

But what can I do? Sometimes what people ask me for isn't what they need. Did Nadia *need* to be popular? Did Florence Nightingale *need* that little bit of extra money she asked for? Did Abraham Lincoln *need* all of those toy soldiers?

And most of the time, what people want isn't what will really make them happy. But they don't ever ask me about that.

Chapter 22
"Nothing Matters Anymore"
by Nadia

The only real purpose for school is to create kid misery. I guess adults figure that everyone should suffer. I've certainly done my share. I would like to be dismissed.

Luckily, Genny told me the story that the cheerleaders were spreading around school. Somehow, they've made this whole fiasco out to be my fault. What kind of people are they, anyway? How dare they make it look like I'm the mean one! They can't even own up to their own cruelty, so they pin it all on someone else. I realize now that they probably never liked me much — or else I wouldn't have had to prove myself to them. Or maybe they don't like *anybody* much, and that's how they treat the people they do call friends. I think it's pretty sad either way. I am surprisingly not all that concerned about them. I mean, who cares? My social status might suffer from not being cool with them, but emotionally I'll be fine. I honestly won't miss them much. Actually, I already feel less stressed, because I don't have anybody to impress anymore. That's what happens when you're double-doomed like me. How many kids can be totally hated by the popular kids and the Einsteins at the same time? Somehow, I've done both with ease.

Isn't life beautiful?

I tried to fake a stomachache and stay home from school today. Nobody bought it, not even Genny. So I had to go to school on the bus — Frieda's mom sure wasn't taking me. Just to save some face, I dressed like a queen in all of my too-awesome Genny clothes. At least if I had to go, I could look great while I was there. Not even fashion could save me, though. I arrived and made a mad dash to a bathroom in the back of the school. I was late to first period because I didn't want to endure any morning harassment at my locker. Those bird-chirping boys were bound to be there ready and willing to eat me alive.

I made a poor attempt at hiding out all day. I didn't want anyone from any group to see me. I stayed in the bathroom stalls between periods, crept into the back of classes at the last second possible, and spent lunchtime holed up in my math teacher's classroom pretending that I desperately needed help with isosceles triangles.

But no matter what I did, people still found me and fried me alive.

Chris saw me in the hallway and made eye contact. He shook his head, obviously disappointed in me, then walked the other way. He had snubbed me — one of the kindest-hearted guys in the school had snubbed me. I couldn't begin to imagine what he was thinking. If he really believed what he had heard, our long conversations outside my house were over. There would be no more laughing together in the cafeteria. I knew that he wouldn't want to go with me to cool parties. Not that I would be invited to them. Plus, he would probably go out of his way to avoid me from now on. At that moment, I was sad. Even if he was crushing on someone else, I adored him just as my friend.

I didn't try to speak to him and defend myself. It was a lost cause. He was such a sweet, sensitive soul. He was probably wretching over the fact that he used to be kinda-sorta close to a girl who turned out to be a savage social beast. If only he knew the truth.

The only other person I cared about was Gretchen. In math class, she asked me what happened. I was too afraid to take on all of her friends, so I just said, "It's not what you think." If I told her the truth, Kelly and her crew would be after me. I hoped one day Gretchen would know everything. All she said was, "I still need your story about the swim team ASAP." Great, that's just what I needed right then — that old assignment requiring me to say good stuff about a losing swim team. My life was awful. Not to mention that Gretchen considered me wanna-be scum of the earth. She dashed out of the classroom two seconds before the bell rang, obviously trying to avoid me. I definitely couldn't be in drama club now. I knew my career on the newspaper would be over, too. But worst of all, I would miss her friendship. She was cool.

Frieda and Matthew tormented me silently. I had given Matthew my school picture a few weeks ago, and he had drawn devil horns out of my head and returned it to me. I found it inside my locker right before last period. Also, Frieda had returned the CDs she had borrowed from me. And even worse, she put the Atari I had given her for her birthday in my locker. There was a note attached to it that read, *Please take this back. I can't look at it. It hurts too much to be reminded of you.* My heart was so broken over how I had stomped on her and taken her for granted. She didn't deserve any of this.

But I didn't, either. This whole situation was totally unfair.

How can you go from the latest greatest thing one day to an embarrassing gossip topic the next? Regardless, I didn't feel like the school freak this time. I didn't have any sort of notion that anyone was better or worse than me anymore. I just felt like we all were what we were: thirteen-year-olds, for better or for worse. Whether we were popular or not.

I wrote the swimming story, with Genny's help. I was tired of lying, so I didn't go on and on about how great the team was. I simply wrote what Genny suggested, something truthful that I believed in. The piece was all about what it takes to be a good swim team. I focused on what winning teams do, stuff like cheering one another on, practicing until they get better and better. I gave pointers from winning coaches on the other things the guys' team needed to do to improve. I needed to follow that kind of advice to become a better friend. No matter what it is we want to do, we're all still learning.

The story came out a few days later. I got some weird stares from the guys. I'm sure they didn't know what to think. But for once, I didn't care. I was finally doing things that felt right for me.

Chapter 23
"I Am Ms. Fix-it"
by Genny the Genie

Thank my holy Throttle that Nadia's popularity took a turn for the worse. I hated the thought that I had created a monster.

I expected what came next. I could have scripted the entire conversation. Nadia came home from school moody and sad. She wasn't the old I'm-nothing Nadia I found when I met her; but she wasn't the new Nadia with all of the fancy clothes, either.

"I'm not one bit happy," she said to me when she walked in the door.

"Have a pillow, girl-*amie*," I said as I patted the bed. "What happened?" I could have guessed, but I thought that would be rude.

She told me about Chris, Gretchen, and the birdcall guys. She said she was sad about Frieda and Matthew.

"Can I have the Atari?" I asked. I mean, I didn't want it to go to waste.

"Genny! Aren't you listening to me?"

"Yes, that's why I asked for the Atari. Are you gonna use it?"

"GENNY!"

"What?"

"It's Frieda's! Aren't you going to help me make things better with her?"

"I can probably do that."

"And what about the rest of my goofed-up life? What are you going to do about that?"

I knew the blame would be put on me — I was expecting it. Humans always think their messes are *all* my fault. "Go on," I said, knowing she needed to vent.

"I asked you to make me popular, and what did you do?"

"I made you popular."

"You made me popular for, like, two seconds. Now I'm worse off than when I started."

"I disagree," I replied.

"You would. And what about Chris? I asked you to hook me up with him, now he hates my guts. You're not a very good genie. That's what I think."

Now she was out of line. "You wait one second, Miss Genie Hater. . . ." It was time for my big speech. "I did what you told me to do. I made you popular. What you decide to do with your life after that is up to you. It's not my fault you let it make you miserable. It's not my fault you were so insensitive to your cousin. It's not like you asked *me* what I thought about the girls you were becoming friends with."

"You wouldn't have known anything about them."

"You should have asked me. Always assume that I know more than you think. I have my ways." That's when I 'fessed up and told her what I knew about Chris's friends. I fibbed a bit — I told her Catfish had overheard one of Chris's phone conversations. But he had described Kelly, Christie, Shapezee, and Whitney in detail.

"Oh, my goodness. He was so right. What did he say about Gretchen?"

"That she's amazing and real, and he adores her."

"Oh, I should have known. . . . Oh, why didn't I see it? He has always liked her, hasn't he?"

"Not like that. They're practically brother and sister — their moms are close friends."

"Oh," Nadia said with a faint smile that quickly turned into a frown. "It doesn't matter anyway, they both hate me now. And I can't believe I tried so hard to be friends with those girls just to impress him. I did everything wrong — everything. I am an idjit."

"You have to learn the hard way. I can't do that for you. I wish I could."

"Oh, that makes me feel better. How did everything get to be such a mess?"

Nadia was teary-eyed and wallowing in self-pity. I can't stand to see people like that because then they don't think straight. So I stupidly said, "We still have time, Nadia. And I'm still your genie. Now, tell me, what do you want me to do?" We actually didn't have time; the twenty-eight days were running out. I have no idea why I say things like that. I guess I just wanted to ease her worries.

"I want you to make me happy."

My head pounded. That was the hardest type of request she could give me. How was I going to do all that in three days or less? Oh, donkey feathers! Oh, tails on birds! Catfish hissed at me, giving me his disapproving look. My heart fluttered with anxiety while my mind raced through the what-to-dos.

The only thing that made me feel kinda-sorta better was this: At least Nadia finally realized that popularity wasn't what she wanted all along. She just wanted friends, fun, and companionship with that cutie Chris. Nadia wanted happiness. That doesn't spring from wells, you know. I just wish we could have skipped the whole popularity thing and gotten down to business earlier.

"Get me some junk food, and we'll get down to business." I wanted to stall her so I could think like Da Vinci for a minute. It took me a few minutes, but I came up with a pretty good plan.

"Here you go," Nadia said, handing me Jolly Ranchers and Sun Chips.

"Thanks . . . Okay," I said, stuffing my face with yummy junk-foodness. "I don't promise that these will make you popular," I added.

"Who cares about popularity anymore?"

Then I told her my plan.

"But what if it doesn't work?" Nadia asked me.

"Don't worry, girl-*amie* — it'll work." I just hoped she couldn't tell how nervous I was when I said that.

We sat down on the computer and started sending electronic cards to Frieda, Matthew, Gretchen, and Chris. There was a red rose on the front of the greeting, and when you clicked on it, it said:

you don't know how much you mean to me. i ask for you to reconsider what you've heard.

kysa knows the truth. but for my part in what
happened, i'm sorry. i never, ever meant to hurt
someone.

i miss you,
nadia

Chapter 24
"I Am Nadia, Here Me Roar"
by Nadia

Forget fashion froufrou. I loved Genny's killer clothes, but they were so not me. She agreed. So we whipped up some more Nadia-like threads. I am most comfortable in black because that's what I've worn all my life in Brooklyn. So now I have little black skirts and tops that I wear with the other up-to-the-minute colorful stuff. I definitely feel like it suits me better. And Genny agrees.

I shouldn't have gotten mad at my genie yesterday — but I couldn't help it. I just can't take all of these changes in my life. First, I leave my hometown and come to this country place. I had to say good-bye to all of my friends. Then I had to endure severe geek abuse at my new school. After that, I got a genie! All of a sudden, I'm popular, then, all of a sudden, I'm back where I started from. I tried to tell Genny that it's no wonder I'm a nutcase.

But I'm a stronger person because of all of this mess. I am *not* saying I'm happy as a clam — I don't know if I'm happy at all. I *am* saying that I've learned a lot.

So starting this morning, I made some changes. I ignored what the birdcallers said, or at least tried to. I put in earplugs — that was Genny's idea, so I wouldn't hear whispers or any mean nothings that people might say about me. I held my head high — and I refused to spend the day hiding in the bathroom.

I wore my Queen Elizabeth barrettes and told myself over and over, "I rule. I am awesome. I am just as good — if not better — than every kid here." I had to stay psyched all day. That's what Genny told me to do. I wanted to stop the awful social cycle that had made me nothing and everything and nothing again — for weeks. I didn't want to be a slave to it for another second.

I just wanted to be happy.

That takes me to the next step: I made my move at lunch. I got a salad with boiled eggs so I'd have extra energy to get through the super-hard day. I walked past the popular table and acted calm and cool. The same old silly girls cackled when I went by. They sounded so ridiculous to me now. Chris's head was down, and I couldn't help noticing that he looked sad. I swear I think I heard Gretchen say, "Hi, Nadia," but I couldn't quite tell with my earplugs in. I took them out, but didn't hear her voice again. I thought there was no way she'd say hello to me — but I hoped she did. I missed her.

Matthew and Frieda were in sight. I could see them and the Einsteins sticking straws up their noses and laughing. I didn't care how embarrassing they were, I was going over there. Frieda is my cousin and I love her.

I stood over the table holding my tray.

"Alien creature at two o'clock," announced an Einstein named Norman. Matthew looked at me and put his head down. Frieda stared into my eyes — reminding me of a puppy who just needed some love.

"May I sit here?" I said.

"I don't think that's — " Matthew started to say just as Frieda hit him on the shoulder.

"Sure," Frieda said. Thankfully, the rest of the Einsteins were quiet. They're much more human than Kelly and her AYM hyenas. They even scooted down to let me sit next to my cousin.

I put a red rose on her plate and said, "I'm sorry." She sniffled. I think she was about to cry

—I didn't mean to hurt her even more right there in front of her friends. I grabbed her hand, which was underneath the table on her knee. "Frieda, I'm so sorry."

"You have no idea how you've made me feel," she said.

"Maybe I don't," I told her. "But I've been hurting a lot lately, too. I don't want to hurt you anymore. I want us to be friends like we used to be."

"I don't think I believe you."

"Frieda, please try. I am sorry. What can I do to make it up to you?"

"Nothing. Just sit here for a while."

So I sat there and had lunch, pushing every bite past the lump in my throat. Matthew was very disapproving. I could tell he was shooting me unsure glances. Finally, the rest of the Einsteins resumed their conversation about how far you can push a straw up your nose before you do permanent damage. Frieda and I sat there in silence for a while, just holding hands under the table. Then she started telling me about how she'd been.

I heard Shapezee making total fun of me. I could hear Kelly saying terrible things loudly across the lunchroom. Something stirred in me —I got steamed-up mad! I got up from the table and walked over to her.

All eyes — from Einsteins to cool kids — were on me. I didn't care.

"What do *you* want?" Kelly asked even more loudly.

"I want *you* to *know* that I can't stand you."

"Good, I can't stand you, either. In fact, I think most people will agree."

"No, most people don't agree. You may be popular, but everyone knows you're a mean-spirited, spoiled brat."

"Spare me."

"You're not worth sparing, Kelly the Queen," I said, remembering her birthday cupcakes. She gave me an evil look. "If being popular means being friends with you, I hope I'm *never* popular."

"Don't worry, you won't be."

"Good, then that means I won't be squirming around on your level." I shot a look at Kysa. "By the way, Kysa knows the truth about the try-outs. You set me up, and you set Frieda up. You like to devastate people just for the fun of it. You're sick."

There was silence. Then Kysa mumbled, "It's true."

"What!?" Kelly screamed.

"What Nadia is saying is true. *All of it.*"

A fight ensued at their table, and I walked

away from it, back to my spot at the Einsteins' table. They were clearly impressed with my speech. I did it for Frieda as much as I did it for myself. I hoped she could see that.

Then, out of the corner of my eye, I saw something amazing happen. Kysa got up from their table and headed our way. Gretchen and Chris followed her. They ended up sitting with me and the Einsteins. Wow, huh? Finally, the rest of the girls shut their mouths.

The rest of the day was just a day. The only difference was in how I felt, which was great. I had done the right thing — I knew that in my heart. Whoever Nadia is, I was finding her.

So I got on the bus after school and headed home to tell Genny everything. I wanted to see what else she could help me do before she left. She has the most amazing ideas. They may sound crazy at first, but they work.

But it was like a movie when I got off the bus near my house. I swear I heard love songs in the background. Chris was standing there — it looked like he was waiting for someone. Turns out, that someone was me.

"Hi," he said, looking at me, then at his feet.

I looked around behind me. He couldn't be speaking to me! "Me?" I asked.

"Yes, you. Nadia from New York."

"Is everything okay?" I asked. I was dying to find out why he and Gretchen left the lunch table.

"Oh, yeah, I guess so. Could we talk for a while?"

"Sure," I said happily. I'd talk to Chris from there to eternity. We took a walk to the neighborhood park.

"I think I've been wrong about you," he told me.

"I didn't set up Frieda — or do any of the other things those girls said I did."

"I know."

"You do?" I asked.

"Yeah, I know none of that was your fault."

"Who told you? What changed your mind?"

"Oh, I don't know. I just believe your side of the story, that's all. Gretchen isn't mad at you, either. She's going to call you tonight."

"Really!" I was filled with happiness to hear that.

"Yeah."

"Oh, great! I really miss her."

"Yeah, she's great, huh?"

Chris and I talked for a long time. He told me that he just couldn't handle his old friends anymore. He said that enough was enough. He told me all about the terrible things they were saying about me and the Einsteins at lunch, and that was the last straw. He told me he was through with them forever.

"I haven't liked them for a long time," he said.

"Really?"

"Really — I just didn't know how to make new friends. Gretchen felt a bit trapped, too. It can be scary to leave behind what you know really well."

"Tell me about it."

"But we've decided that we're glad we've met you. Kysa said it, too. We are more comfortable when we're hanging around with you."

Our conversation was wonderful. It was like we couldn't stop talking. Everything was clicking. If he wasn't so in love with another girl, I would have grabbed his hand. I just felt like I belonged with him — whether we were meant to be just friends or more, I didn't know.

"Did you ever figure out who she was?" I asked Chris.

"No," he replied sadly. "And I don't think I'll ever see her again."

Yes! I thought. *That gives me a chance!* We walked home, having a heart-to-heart the whole way.

Chapter 25
"Chris and Nadia Are Supercute"
by Genny the Genie

"Genny, I want someone to meet you," I heard from outside Nadia's bedroom door. I was busy watching *The Simpsons*.

"Yay! Nadia's home!" I said.

Then she walked in with Chris on her arm. Our eyes met; we both were shocked. Why did he have to be the *one* person she chose to reveal me to?

What was I supposed to do? Nadia could not know the truth!

"You?" Chris said.

I didn't say anything. I didn't know what to do — especially since he was finally starting to like Nadia again. The worst thing that could happen was for him to remember his feelings for me. *Think fast, think fast!* I was freaking out. I fiddled with my hair. I didn't look them in the eyes. I nervously walked over to fiddle with the CD player. Without even thinking, I put on a hard-core rap album. The whole scene was psycho.

"Do you two know each other?" Nadia asked, obviously confused. "You can't know her — she's, um, my cousin from France." I knew Nadia couldn't exactly say I'm a genie without Chris thinking she's crazy. But still, oh my — this whole scene was sticks.

Then it hit me — I knew what I had to do. "Oh, Nadia, it's just a French thing. He doesn't *really* know me." Chris was giving me that I-love-you grin. His eyes were glossing over, and he was remembering our time together. I had to think fast — I didn't want Nadia to know I had liked him. Or worse, how much he had liked me.

"Oh, Chris. I'm so glad you came! You can help me decide which designer outfit to wear! I have so many, I just don't know what to do!"

"Huh?" he said.

"What? You can't help me pick something out? Humph!"

"Genny! What's going — " Nadia tried to ask.

"What do you mean what is going on? Not that you would know it because you weren't

145

here, but Jodi on *Days of Our Deaths* died today, and I cried my eyes out! I mean, it was tragic!"

"Who? What are you talking about?"

"I am just telling you that I've had a *très* tough day. Please don't make it more stressful. Do you have to bring people over? And, oh, could you please get me some pepperoni pizza, Nadia? Catfish and I are *stahhh-ving*," I asked as I flipped my hair and put on some lip gloss.

"Well, Genny, I'm kinda busy."

"I DON'T CARE!!! I'm hungry, and I WANT FOOD NOW!" The look in Chris's eyes left immediately! It was working. *Whew! What a relief!* What could I do if he didn't buy it? I was pretty proud of my bratty, self-absorbed antics, if I do say so myself.

"You're unbelievable," Nadia said. She was mad at me, I could tell. But I knew I could make it up to her later. "C'mon, Chris, we're leaving. She's lost it."

"Bring me some pizza on your way back," I demanded as she shut her bedroom door.

"I'm really sorry about my genie," Nadia told Chris as she walked down the steps.

"What a snot!" I heard him say. "You're way too sweet to hang out with her, Nadia."

I laid back on the bed and smiled. I'm a pretty clever genie, if I do say so myself!

The boy wasn't mine, he was Nadia's. So it didn't matter whether he was my dear French Frederick or not.

I never really had a chance.

Chapter 26
"Where Would I Be Without Genny?"
by Nadia

Genny lost it last night. I have no idea what that little bratty act was all about. She told me she'd gotten bad news through genie-mail. Whatever! I don't get her sometimes. At least when I got back home things were back to normal.

"Do you like Chris? Did he kiss you? Tell me! Tell me!"

"You know I like Chris, are you crazy?"

"What about the kiss? Did he?"

I smiled smugly . . . and shrugged my shoulders.

"He did! He did!" Genny said. She was way too excited. I swear, genies can be mucho moody.

I told her the story. It was beautiful. We went to his house, and he showed me around. Then he said he had something special for me to see. He opened the door to his room, and there it was: his wonderful photo collection. He is truly talented. He takes black-and-white pictures of rotting trees, but somehow he makes them seem beautiful. After seeing his photos, I liked him about ten times more — if that's possible — than I did before. He told me to sit down, and he rooted through some things. Then he handed me a picture. It was of a daisy.

"Genny, how did he know I loved them? Isn't that freaky?"

"Oh, I don't think so. I think it means you were meant to be," she said sadly.

Then, like I told Genny, Chris kissed me. I had the picture in my hand. I was speechless. I couldn't believe *he'd* want to give it to *me*. I told her that he held my face with his hands as our lips moved closer and closer together. It was the most meaningful moment of my whole entire life.

"I knew he'd fall for you," Genny told me while I smiled somewhat stupidly. "I knew it!"

"Genny, thank you thank you thank you! I am so happy. Not just because of him. But just because. I found my place at school. I have some friends — only a few, but that's enough. And I don't worry about what other people say or think. I'm happy! And I have Chris! So I'm more than happy." I went on and on; I couldn't help it.

Genny didn't say anything. She just smiled and hugged me. I asked her what was wrong, because she looked so sad. She only said she was happy for me. Then she went over to my CD player and put on her favorite Madonna music. We danced around the room. At the time, I didn't realize it would be our last dance.

"Genny, since you still have tonight, do you think we can squeeze in one more wish?"

"Sure, little potato. Sure."

I have no idea why she calls me such strange things — but when she says them, they're very sweet.

"Well, I want something for Frieda."

"Yes."

"Is there any way we can hook her up with the man of her dreams?"

"Who?"

"Matthew!"

"Oh, I have an idea!" Genny said. How does she come up with them so fast? "Invite them over!"

I called Frieda and asked her to stop by — I knew Matthew would be with her. I wanted to tell Frieda all about my kiss with Chris, and I knew she'd be dying to hear everything. At

first, I felt funny saying it in front of Matthew —
who by the way, was wearing plaid, old-man
golfing pants. But ever since my last fight
with Frieda, he seemed totally, completely over
me. So it was okay, I guess. If you ask me, his
concern for Frieda was more than just friendship. My whole shenanigan just seemed to
bring them closer — which was great, if you
ask me.

Genny totally agreed. Matthew and Frieda
just needed one more extra push into couple-
dom. So Genny put mistletoe — it was nowhere
near the holidays, mind you — right above my
doorway. She wanted me to confront them
when they walked in. I chatted them up first to
make sure everyone was comfortable. They
looked cozy and cuddly with each other, but I
knew no love words had been spoken.

And they clearly needed to be.

So I left my room, making a lame excuse that
I had to get us all a soft drink. As I left, I said,
"Come here, you two, I want to show you
something."

They walked toward me, just underneath the
mistletoe.

"Look up," I pointed. "That means you have
to kiss. And if you ask me, a smooch between
you two is long overdue."

I left them there for a while, knowing they needed to have a serious conversation.

It was almost an hour before I heard them barreling down the steps.

"Thanks, Nadia," Frieda whispered in my ear. They walked out the door hand in hand.

I love being a matchmaker!

I went back to my room, and Genny and I laughed and danced. She had to leave me the next morning, so she told me to e-mail her to keep her posted on all of the new romantic developments.

I wrote her over and over again — telling her about Chris and me and Frieda and Matthew. I wanted to tell her how great we were all doing, and how we owed it all to her. But the e-mails I sent kept coming back to me.

She was gone.

I will miss her forever.

I listen to my Madonna CD a lot lately, and I dance around, pretending she is still with me.

Chapter 27
A Bittersweet Bye-bye
by Genny, you know,
the Genie

I left without a lot of fanfare. We danced in Nadia's room. We ate lots of junk food — even Nadia did. And she finally gave Catfish what he wanted — a couple of pats on the head.

Then *poof*! My twenty-eight days were up.

I hugged Nadia and told her good-bye. She was sad to see me go, I could tell. But she also had a gleam in her eye. She was on her way over to Chris's. She's happy with me and the job I've done. I know because she told me so.

I hate good-byes. I always try to make them as happy and pleasant as possible. After all, there's no reason for me *and* my clients to be drowning in self-pity.

Sometimes, like this time, I wanted to stay. I liked Nadia's friends. I felt at home in her bedroom. I could get used to going to her school and taking classes like she does.

I just want to be human so badly — but I can't admit that to anybody. I can't tell a lot of people my true feelings, because they don't know what it's like to be a genie.

It's lonely.

But I stay because I get to make the world a better place — one Nadia at a time.

About the Author

Kristen Kemp is the author of several books about Genny the Genie, as well as other Scholastic titles, such as the 2 Grrrls guides. She stays busy writing for women's and teen magazines and is currently a contributing editor at *YM*. She lives in Saratoga Springs, NY, with her husband, Steve, their dog, Clipper, and two cats. In her spare time, she loves to visit her hometown in Indiana.